The Infancy Gospels of Jesus

Apocryphal Tales from the Childhoods of Mary and Jesus— Annotated & Explained

Translation and Annotation by
Stevan Davies

Foreword by A. Edward Siecienski, PhD

Walking Together, Finding the Way ®
SKYLIGHT PATHS®
PUBLISHING

The Infancy Gospels of Jesus:
Apocryphal Tales from the Childhoods of Mary and Jesus—Annotated & Explained

Library of Congress Cataloging-in-Publication Data
The infancy Gospels of Jesus : apocryphal tales from the childhoods of Mary and Jesus, annotated & explained / translation and annotation by Stevan Davies ; foreword by A. Edward Siecienski.—Quality pbk. ed.
       p. cm.
   Includes bibliographical references (p.   ).
   ISBN 978-1-59473-258-4 (quality pbk.)
   ISBN-13: 978-1-68336-381-1 (hc)
   1. Apocryphal infancy Gospels. I. Davies, Stevan L., 1948– II. Protevangelium
Jacobi. English. III. Gospel of the infancy. English. IV. Gospel of Thomas (Infancy
Gospel) English.
   BS2850.A3I54 2009
   229'.8—dc22
                                                                    2009008927

Manufactured in the United States of America
Cover design: Tim Holtz
Cover art: © iStockphoto.com/Jaroslaw Baczewski

SkyLight Paths Publishing is creating a place where people of different spiritual traditions come together for challenge and inspiration, a place where we can help each other understand the mystery that lies at the heart of our existence.

SkyLight Paths sees both believers and seekers as a community that increasingly transcends traditional boundaries of religion and denomination—people wanting to learn from each other, *walking together, finding the way.*

SkyLight Paths, "Walking Together, Finding the Way," and colophon are trademarks of LongHill Partners, Inc., registered in the U.S. Patent and Trademark Office.

Walking Together, Finding the Way
Published by SkyLight Paths Publishing
An Imprint of Turner Publishing Company
4507 Charlotte Avenue, Suite 100
Nashville, TN 37209
Tel: (615) 255-2665
www.skylightpaths.com

Contents □

Foreword □

by A. Edward Siecienski, PhD

Whenever I teach introductory courses in Christian theology, I allot time to the Church's doctrines concerning Mary—the Council of Ephesus's affirmation that she was the Theotokos ("God bearer") as well as the Roman Catholic dogmas of the Immaculate Conception and Assumption. Although the latter teachings sometimes raise questions in the minds of my Protestant students, it is the doctrine of Mary's three-fold virginity that elicits the strongest reaction and, often enough, the strangest looks. It is one thing to believe Mary conceived as a virgin (*virginitas ante partum*), but quite another to accept that she remained a virgin unto death (*virginitas post partum*) When I try to explain the third aspect of Mary's virginity, the concept of *virginitas in partu* (i.e., that she remained a virgin even in the process of giving birth), students move beyond simple incredulity. Many of them just laugh, as if I had told some sort of joke. I assure them that I am serious, and that this is a teaching of both the Catholic and the Orthodox Churches. They ask, "Where did this come from? It's not in the Bible, is it?" I reply, "Not exactly," and begin reading from the Protoevangelion of James (which has also been called the Gospel of James) and the story of the unbelieving maidservant Salome.

Perhaps no other apocryphal book has been as influential on Church teaching (especially in the Orthodox and Catholic traditions) as the Protoevangelion of James. "Despite its condemnation in official documents, it has dominated the development of the Marian legend, providing much of the basic material for Mary's biography."[1] The Orthodox liturgy regularly invokes the prayers of "the holy ancestors of God, Joachim and Anna."[2] Mary's birth is celebrated in both the East and the West, as is the feast of her Entrance (Presentation) in the Temple. Icons of the Nativity, which adorn churches throughout the world, regularly show Mary and child in a cave, with midwives and an aged Joseph nearby. The basis for all these prayers, feasts, and iconic representations is the Protoevangelion of James.

Many of the fathers of the Church were familiar with the Protoevangelion and referenced it freely. Justin Martyr (famous for his second century *Apology*) may have used it, and the great third century exegete Origen of Alexandria explicitly mentions it to support the belief that the "brothers of Jesus" were children of Joseph by his first wife. The Byzantine hymnographer Romanos the Melodist closely followed the narrative of the Protoevangelion in his *Hymn on the Birth of Mary* and recent scholarship has begun to look more carefully at the influence of James on later Mariological piety, especially in the eighth century.[3] Even as late as the fourteenth century, Gregory Palamas, Metropolitcan of Thessalonica and defender of hesychasm, utilized the Protoevangelion for his homilies on the feasts of the Theotokos.[4]

Yet despite its widespread use (especially in the Christian East), by the late fifth century, the *Gelasian Decree* listed the Protoevangelion among the apocryphal books to be avoided by believing Christians.[5] This is in many ways understandable, especially given its mid- to late-second-century origin, which would have failed to meet two of the necessary criteria for inclusion in the canon—apostolicity and antiquity. Yet the orthodoxy of the Protoevangelion did not seem to be at issue, as the Church continued to rely on it as the basis for certain liturgical celebrations and teachings concerning the Mother of God.

The same cannot be said about the Infancy Gospel of Thomas, a book that even today shocks and surprises the pious Christian reader. Christians remember Jesus as the loving savior who healed the sick and raised the dead. To read about a petulant, all-powerful child who regularly struck down and blinded those who crossed him is to be confronted with another Christ. And even though elements of the book have made their way into Christian art (not to mention the Qur'an [5:110]), the Infancy

Gospel of Thomas does not even come close to the Protoevangelion in terms of its impact.

Up to now there have been few works on the infancy gospels that were both scholarly and accessible. True, there was a recent brief period (post-*Da Vinci Code*) when numerous works on the apocrypha appeared, but most were attempts (and remarkably poor ones at that) to show how these books chronicled the "true history" of Jesus suppressed by the Church. Thus I was quite happy when Stevan Davies told me he was writing a book on the infancy gospels, and genuinely honored when he asked me to write the Foreword. Stevan Davies's previous books on the apocrypha, along with his studies of the canonical New Testament, are well known and respected by scholars. If anyone could fill this gap in biblical studies, I knew Steve could do it.

On a personal level, this book brought back many fond memories of my years working with Steve at Misericordia University in Pennsylvania, sitting at lunch or in his office discussing (and often disputing) theological matters. Even when we had to "agree to disagree" about something, I walked away from each encounter respecting him all the more for his quick wit, intellect, and commitment to sound scholarship. My guess is that readers of this book will have the same experience. The infancy gospels are incredibly interesting and remarkably influential texts. For those familiar with them, and for those encountering them for the first time, herein lies a study well worth reading.

Introduction □
Tales from the Childhood of Mary and Jesus

The infancy gospels are collections of stories from nearly two thousand years ago that let us share the miraculous world of the young Christ Jesus as Christians of the earliest centuries of the church imagined that world to be. The infancy gospels are not, strictly speaking, only about the infancies of Mary and Jesus. Rather, these ancient narratives tell stories about the circumstances of their conceptions, their births, their infancies, and their childhoods. In the infancy gospels we hear about the early life of Jesus's mother Mary, about marvelous events that accompanied the birth of Jesus, about the holy family's journeys throughout Egypt, and especially about Jesus's life as a boy in Nazareth. These stories are fictions, legends, folktales arising out of the imaginations of ordinary Christians of the second through the fifth centuries. In this book we will be discussing three infancy gospels, the earliest surviving examples of the type: the Gospel of James, the Gospel of the Infancy, and the Infancy Gospel of Thomas. They are very different from each other in form and content and so they need to be considered separately.

The Gospel of James and the Infancy Gospel of Thomas probably originated in the later part of the second century, and the Gospel of the Infancy from a period several centuries later still, perhaps toward the end of the fourth century. The stories the three works tell fit together chronologically, and they will be discussed in chronological sequence in this book: the Gospel of James tells about the birth and life of Mary up to the time of Jesus's birth, which it describes in a distinct and beautiful fashion; the Gospel of the Infancy retells that story of Jesus's birth with interesting variations, and then it gives a fascinating series of stories of Jesus as a babe in arms as his family traveled in Egypt and then in Judea; the Infancy Gospel of Thomas traces Jesus's boyhood in Nazareth from when he was only three up to age twelve. The Gospel of James is primarily focused on Mary rather than Jesus himself, and it is particularly interested in showing how Mary maintained her purity for her whole youthful life. The Gospel of the Infancy is principally a series of folktales featuring the miraculous power of the infant Jesus.

Some readers may be shocked at aspects of the Infancy Gospel of Thomas, for supposedly in his earliest years, Jesus actually used his divine powers to injure some of those who offended him, but as the tales go on Jesus learns to use his powers for good. As a whole, the Infancy Gospel of Thomas is an extraordinary set of stories that show how an infant incarnation of God began to learn to control his supernatural powers, and how his neighbors in Nazareth responded to his powers and his personal growth, first with fear, then with admiration.

In most of the documents that survive from the early centuries of the Christian church we read the work of well-educated men whose voices are not those of the common people. When ordinary people spoke about their Christian religion, they spoke in stories, legends, and tales of active divine power. No one will say that the infancy stories are historically factual, and hardly anyone will argue that they are crucial to Christian belief, but they do remain interesting because they give us great insight into the ordinary Christian people's religious thoughts and imagination.

I will now discuss the three infancy gospels briefly in this introduction and then, in subsequent chapters, annotate and explain each of them in much more detail as we read the tales themselves.

The Gospel of James and the Birth of Mary

Today Christmas is the greatest celebration of the Christian religion. People who never otherwise go to church can be found in evening Christmas services. If in theory Easter takes precedence because the grace brought about by the death and resurrection of Christ should take precedence over his birth, in the actual practice of Christian cultures the celebration of Jesus's birth is the foremost festival of all. Christmas represents the arrival of God on earth, the coming down of divinity into human form, and so it signifies the breaking of boundaries between the profane world and the heavens.

In the earliest Christian centuries, Jesus's birth was of such great importance that stories from outside the canonical gospel tradition began to be told about how the incarnate God arrived here. The stories continued to form and evolve as they were told and retold. Christians speculated that if the greatest event in history had been the arrival of God's incarnation in Jesus, then the greatest woman in history must have been the mother through whom Jesus came. As the story of her virginity in motherhood came to be part of Christian doctrine, stories arose that stressed the purity of her life—from her birth through the climactic events of an elaborate Christmas story somewhat different than the one told in the Bible. These stories and traditions came together toward the end of the second century in an account called the Gospel of James.

The Gospel of James begins by describing Mary's parents and the events leading to her birth. Then it gives an account of her life up to the Annunciation. Finally, through a long and beautifully written narrative, it tells of the birth of Jesus and Herod's persecution of the babies of Bethlehem. This is not a historical account but a set of legends that came from the folktale traditions of ordinary and mostly illiterate Christian people. The Gospel of James is an example of folk religion, the religion of the common people.

MARY'S PARENTS: SAINT JOACHIM AND SAINT ANNE

As tales were told, sometimes their characters came to life in Christian tradition. Mary's parents are never mentioned in the Bible, however, through the influence of the Gospel of James, where Mary's parents are given the names Joachim and Anne, these two legendary persons came to be honored in both the Catholic and Orthodox churches. In Hebrew the name of Mary's mother would have been "Hannah," in Greek it is

"Anna," and in English it is "Anne." So, in this book, we will use "Anne" for her name. Today, in the Orthodox churches, Joachim and Anne have September 9 as their feast day; in the Roman Catholic churches the date is July 26. Saint Anne is said to be the patroness of women in labor and Saint Joachim is known as the patron of grandparents.

Mary's early life needed to be located somewhere, and so traditions arose placing Mary's birth and infancy in the capital of Judea, Jerusalem, where Anne and Joachim supposedly made their home. Her girlhood, though, was not spent at home. According to the Gospel of James, she was admitted into the Jerusalem Temple, where she lived, fed by angels of God, until puberty.

Today, in the Old City of Jerusalem, if you walk down the Via Dolorosa toward the Lion's Gate, with the sacred area of the Dome of the Rock on your right and the Muslim residential quarter on your left, you'll notice a stone doorway with the words "BIRTH PLACE of the VIRGIN MARY" painted above it. Go inside and a polite man will escort you down flights of stairs carved in stone and through a series of grottos. He will tell you that this was the ancient home of Saints Joachim and Anne, Mary's parents. On the rugged stone walls of the grottos you will see icons in the Orthodox Christian style telling the story of Mary's birth and depicting the day that Mary was delivered to the care of the high priest of the Temple of Jerusalem, which would have been located about a thousand feet to the south of this point.

At the end of the series of grottos you will reach Mary's birthplace, a semicircular cavern marked by a few candles, lilies, and icons above an ancient mosaic floor. The scene looks homemade but it is deeply sincere and even holy. Nearby, a little sign in Greek and English announces that you are standing in the "house of the Righteous Ancestors of God, the parents of the Virgin Mary, Saints Joachim and Anna."[1] It is an astounding idea: Who could possibly be the ancestors of God?

Next door, only yards away, in a spacious walled enclosure that incorporates a large monastery, green lush gardens, and a major archaeological excavation, stands the Roman Catholic church of St. Anne, an ancient crusader-built church dedicated to Jesus's grandmother, a church that has an elegantly simple interior and astoundingly fine acoustics. As you enter, there are stairs to the right that lead down into a different grotto that was, according to its sign in French and English, "The Birthplace of Our Lady." This grotto is brightly illuminated and professionally manufactured. It features a large, brilliantly colored modern painting of the nativity and one traditional icon in Orthodox style that depicts Saint Anne just after giving birth, looking understandably exhausted, just as she does in the very similar icons in the Orthodox grottos next door.

There is one legend and one set of honored saints, but two separate sacred locations claim to have been their dwelling place two thousand years ago. The idea that Anne and Joachim's home was once in Jerusalem near the Temple of God, and the legends about Mary's birth come to us from the Gospel of James. This gospel is particularly important to Orthodox and Catholic Christians because it helped form the foundation for devotion to the Blessed Mother and it gave rise to significant legends that persist, as the Jerusalem shrines prove, up to this day.

THE GOSPEL OF JAMES AND THE CANONICAL TRADITION

The Gospel of James is not an isolated text that simply retells folktales apart from any wider textual history. Rather, the Gospel of James is one of a series of interconnected Christian texts that New Testament scholars call the "synoptic" Gospels. The gospels of Matthew, Mark, and Luke are quite similar, often containing word-for-word identical passages in their original Greek, while John's gospel is quite different and obviously distinct. The synoptic gospels are broadly similar when seen together, which is what the word "synoptic" means. For nearly two centuries now, although various hypotheses have been offered to explain why the synoptic gospels are so similar, the great majority of New Testament scholars have come to agree that the first of the gospels to have been written was Mark and that Matthew and Luke are revised and expanded versions of Mark. The Gospel of James is the continuation of that literary tradition. It is a further revision and expansion of the parts of the other synoptic gospels that tell of Jesus's birth and his family.

Mark's Story In the Gospel of Mark, Jesus's birth is not mentioned at all. We hear nothing of his father, just that Jesus is the "son of Mary," and that he has four brothers—James, Joseph, Judas, and Simon—and several sisters (Mark 6:3). Because the custom of that culture was to call a boy by his father's name after "bar," which means "son of," we would expect to hear of Jesus bar-Joseph, but we do not. We have the Greek equivalent of Jesus bar-Mary, which implies that his father's identity was not known. In Mark's account, Jesus's mother and brothers thought him "outside of himself" and came to take charge of him, only to be repudiated by him in favor of his disciples and other followers (Mark 3:21–35). His family members never again appear in Mark's gospel. There is no hint of a miraculous birth or virginal conception; the portrayal of Mary is minimal and rather negative in Mark's story.

Matthew's Story Ten or twenty years later, when Matthew revised and expanded Mark into his own gospel, he incorporated into it a lengthy collection of Jesus's sayings, appended a short narrative about Jesus's resurrection appearances, and produced a birth story making it clear that Mary was made pregnant while she was engaged to Joseph, but not by Joseph, and that the Holy Spirit gave unqualified approval to her pregnancy. At least, this is how the text is viewed by scholars such as professors Robert Miller of Juniata College[2] and Jane Schaberg of the University of Detroit.[3] They point out that while every Christian for the last two thousand or so years has assumed that a divinely empowered virginal conception is central to Matthew's account, Matthew doesn't actually say that any such thing took place. Rather, Matthew is principally interested in showing that events of Jesus's birth fulfill prophecy, including the prophecy found in Isaiah 7:14 that "a young woman will conceive and bear a son and you will name him Emmanuel," which means "God is with us." Scholars have known for a very long time that the term *almah* in the Hebrew prophecy of Isaiah 7:14 does not mean "virgin" but "young woman," and that the ancient Greek version of the Bible translates *almah* as "parthenos," which also does not necessarily mean "virgin" but can mean just "girl" or "young woman." It may be that Matthew's intention was more to show a fulfillment of the prophecy that Jesus would be "emmanuel" or "God with us" than to describe a virginal conception. If Matthew did have a virginal conception in mind, it is certainly odd that he didn't clearly specify that crucial fact. In contrast, the authors of Luke's and James's gospels take pains to make it very clear indeed.

In addition to showing that Mary's pregnancy was approved by the Holy Spirit, by having that fact declared to Joseph by an angel of God, Matthew constructs a story of visiting magi led by a star and a story of the Herod-mandated slaughter of the infants of Bethlehem. The latter apparently was to demonstrate the fulfillment of a prophecy from Jeremiah (31:15): "In Ramah was there a voice heard, lamentation, and weeping, and great mourning, Rachel weeping for her children, and would not be comforted, because they are not." Matthew believes this passage refers to Herod's murders in Bethlehem. Herod's assault causes Jesus's family to flee to Egypt, which later permits their fulfillment of the prophecy "Out of Egypt I called my son" (Hosea 11:1), when the family returns to Palestine. Matthew's interest in showing the manner of Jesus's birth and early life is mainly to construct a story that shows the fulfillment of various Hebrew prophecies. In the process, Matthew focuses on Joseph as his main character, telling readers of the revelations God gave to Joseph and of Joseph's faithful response to those revelations. Mary is a secondary figure in this account.

Luke's Story Luke seems to have heard Matthew's gospel once (being read-aloud was almost invariably the way that texts were utilized in the ancient world) and, since he owned copies of Matthew's primary sources—the Gospel of Mark and the sayings of Jesus that Matthew used—Luke knew what Matthew had done to produce his own text. Luke concluded that Matthew's revision of Mark through an addition of birth and resurrection-appearance stories could have been done better. Therefore, perhaps twenty years after Matthew's gospel was completed, Luke took up the task of again revising Mark, adding a more extensive story of Jesus's resurrection appearances and a much more complex and expansive narrative of Jesus's birth than Matthew had produced.

While Matthew tells us that Mary was impregnated without Joseph's involvement, and that God's spirit approved of this, Luke unambiguously constructs a story of Mary's divinely empowered virginal impregnation after an angelic annunciation: "'And, behold, you will conceive in your womb, and bring forth a son, and you will name him Jesus.' Mary replied, 'How will this be, seeing I know not a man?' The angel answered, 'The Holy Ghost shall come upon you, and the power of the Highest shall overshadow you: therefore also that holy thing which shall be born of you will be called the Son of God'" (Luke 1:31, 34–35). This account was designed to leave no doubt that a miraculous virginal conception took place. Something that might be inferred from Matthew's account is spelled out in Luke's. Furthermore, although a rather negative view of Mary in Mark's gospel becomes a positive view in Matthew's, neither of these two authors focuses much attention on her. In Luke's birth story, Mary is the focal point and heroine of the whole infancy account.

The birth story as Luke writes it (1:1–2:52), is a self-contained unit— it is the first "infancy gospel" and it marks the beginning of Catholic Christian special devotion to the "blessed virgin Mary." In addition, Luke's two chapters weave the birth of John the Baptist to Elizabeth and Zechariah into its account of the birth of Jesus; the Gospel of James will also do this later on but in significantly different ways.

James's Story The Gospel of James is the next stage in the development of this literary sequence. Mary is introduced in Luke's gospel as a woman who has found such favor with God that she is chosen to bear the Christ child through divine impregnation, but of her earlier life we hear nothing. In James's gospel we hear her own story, how she came to be born and how she came to remain pure enough to bear God's son, and especially how we should be confident that her virginity remained intact prior to, and even after, Jesus's birth. In addition, James integrates Luke's story of the birth of John the Baptist with Matthew's story of Herod's persecution, including a fascinating account of the assassination of John's father, the high priest Zechariah. The author of the Gospel of James uses stories he borrowed from Luke's gospel, stories he took from Matthew's gospel, and stories he learned from followers of John the Baptist to construct a new and significant account. The Gospel of James is a new creative stage in the synoptic tradition.

Some scholars, including myself, have called the Sayings Gospel of Thomas "the fourth synoptic gospel."[4] We were mistaken, because that text is not taking the previously written synoptic gospels and expanding and supplementing them in new directions, which is what the synoptic tradition does. The Sayings Gospel of Thomas is just a list of sayings. In fact, the Gospel of James is "the fourth synoptic gospel," for James has done just what Matthew and Luke did, taking existing written accounts in the same linear narrative tradition and using them to serve his own particular biographical purposes. While the dating of all of the gospels is very unsure, scholars generally date Mark at around 70 CE, Matthew somewhere near 80 to 90 CE, Luke between 90 CE and up to as late as 110 CE, and James in the vicinity of 150 to 175 CE. All were originally written in Greek.

The Mother of God as a Little Girl

Mary is the central character in the first part of the Gospel of James, and her role is to be the vehicle for the incarnation; she is preselected for her role as the Mother of God, and while she is a little girl everyone in the narrative seems to know what her role will be. Her parents construct a pure and inviolate space for her to live in as an infant and then, with the happy encouragement of the Temple priesthood, she moves into the holiest space on earth, the Holy of Holies of the Jerusalem Temple. Several years later, after a sign from God that Joseph is the selected man, she moves into his home where, during his absence, she becomes pregnant with the Son of God. These events display, in one sense, over-the-top adulation for Mary, portraying her as the featured focal point of the Judaism of Jerusalem's Temple and as a crucial element in God's plan. But in another sense, the story isn't really about Mary as a person at all. She is a necessary part of a planned and inevitable sequence of events, culminating in Jesus's birth, and those events are what matter. We are not given any hint that Mary herself has somehow earned the right to be the Mother of God. She is predestined to be Jesus's mother just as Jesus is predestined to be God's Son.

In Luke's gospel, Mary understands her divinely appointed mission and purpose, but in James's gospel it is far from clear that she understands. When she visits and speaks with Elizabeth, her kinswoman, pregnant at the time with the baby who will become John the Baptist, Mary does not recall the angelic explanation of the reason for her own pregnancy. Later on she is not able to tell Joseph how her pregnancy came about. The Gospel of James shows that Mary received messages from an angel about the reason for her pregnancy, but it does not make the assumption that every message from an angel is immediately understood.

As the text moves along Mary matures. She changes from a perfect little girl who is implicitly known by everyone mentioned in the text to be the future Mother of God into a pregnant young virgin woman who does not quite grasp what has happened to her. The author of James is not making a mistake here or writing badly; rather he seems to be intent on giving us a portrayal of Mary in which she matures away from a girlhood of unqualified holiness into a young womanhood marked by some confusion and even embarrassment, for as her pregnancy advances she is said to hide herself from public view.

The author of the Gospel of James frequently uses the sophisticated literary technique of internal monologue, in which readers hear what characters in the narrative think or say to themselves. The Gospel of James focuses first on the thoughts of Mary's father Joachim and her mother Anne. As the story evolves, we hear the musings of her guardian Joseph, and occasionally, even the thoughts of Mary herself. Interestingly, sometimes angelic or divine messages respond to the internal monologues of characters as though God is hearing and responding to what the characters are thinking.

At one point the text changes from third-person narrative, "he did such and such," to first-person narrative, "I did such and such," evidently to focus the reader's attention on an astonishing and beautiful passage where Joseph describes the brief pause in time at the moment of Jesus's birth. On the whole, the Gospel of James is a surprisingly sophisticated literary production, more than just a collection of folktales, although that is where it began. And it is more than a defense of Mary's virginity or a formal text praising Mary's character.

The Gospel of the Infancy

The Gospel of the Infancy is a later production, perhaps fourth or fifth century in date. It does not have the sophistication of the Gospel of James, although in its first section it gives readers a revised and more exalted version of stories taken from the Gospel of James. We are told about the divine and human intermingling of song at the time of Jesus's birth and hear of a vision of Jesus gleaming like a pillar of light when Simeon beholds him in the Temple: We even follow the Zoroastrian magi back to their native Persia and learn about their ceremony in honor of Jesus. It is the same narrative as in the Gospel of James but more elevated and splendid.

The central section of the Gospel of the Infancy is its most interesting part, a series of adventures of the holy family as they travel in exile throughout Egypt. Mary is portrayed as the perfect Blessed Mother, but she lacks the doubts and puzzlement that make her a more human character in the Gospel of James; perfection does not make a character more interesting. Jesus, too, is perfect; he is an infant with divine powers that work entirely automatically. To touch him or to touch something that has touched him gives immediate miraculous results. This collection of tales does not show any change or development in the characters, just one divine thing after another. It is a collection of folktales, some of which are meant to be funny, most of which are meant to be awe-inspiring. There are some lovely passages, especially in the parts that rewrite the Gospel of James, but on the whole, the Gospel of the Infancy is folk literature with little claim to sophistication.

MIRACLES OF JESUS'S PRESENCE

Jesus's powers are so great in the Gospel of the Infancy that just his arrival in town causes the great idols of Egypt to come crashing to the ground. We hear about a mule who is really a bewitched man—he is restored to human form when Mary puts baby Jesus on his back. We hear about the power of Jesus healing a deaf woman, driving the demons out of a boy whom they possessed, and we are told that the scented balsam shrubs of Matariyya, Egypt, originated from droplets of baby Jesus's perspiration that fell from the garments Mary had recently washed in a miraculous spring that Jesus had caused to emerge from the dry ground.

In the central part of the Gospel of the Infancy, Jesus's family moves through Egypt like a conquering army. Their war is between the true God, represented by Jesus, and the false gods of the Egyptians, embodied principally in great statues. It is not the actions of Jesus that destroy the statues and drive the Egyptian gods into exile but his mere presence. Like the ancient ark of the covenant that manifested the presence of the God Yahweh during battles fought by the Israelites, God is present in Jesus. But, just as the ark did not act on its own, neither does the infant Jesus. Rather, Jesus embodies the very presence of God and thereby God's powers act through him.

In later sections of the Gospel of the Infancy, Jesus is more than a babe in arms, as he is throughout the central part; he has become a boy able to move and act and play with others. Some of the stories in the account are meant to be amusing. For example, in one story Jesus and other little boys play hide and seek, Jesus asks some women where his friends have gone and they tell him kiddingly that there are no children around, just some baby goats. Right then and there Jesus changes his playmates into baby goats, though he soon changes them back. This is not profound and deep Christology—it is pure fun.

In reading these tales you can see how the folktale traditions of Europe, known to us today mainly from Disney movies, could have emerged from the folktales told in the ancient world. This book includes a sampling of stories from the Gospel of the Infancy, not the whole text, because the stories become repetitive after a while and much of the latter part of the text duplicates stories found in the Infancy Gospel of Thomas. Where portions have been deleted you will find five dots as an indicator.

We might wonder whether people of ancient times believed that these folktales were historically true. I think not. Just as we today think nothing of suspending our disbelief when reading a novel or watching a television show or a movie, we can easily bring our disbelief back again if required and say, "No, that never really happened." There is no reason to think that ancient hearers of the miraculous journeying of Jesus, Mary, and Joseph didn't do the same thing: suspend disbelief yet have the capacity for skepticism when required.

The Infancy Gospel of Thomas

One of the most extraordinary documents in the whole history of Christianity is the little list of tales known as the Infancy Gospel of Thomas. It was written in Greek in the period 125 CE to 175 CE and is the story of Jesus as a little boy growing up in the village of Nazareth trying to live in human society while at the same time possessing the power of God. It would be easy enough to write an account of Jesus's early life that shows him exercising his powers always for good, moving through Nazareth in an aura of divine perfection, and pleasing everyone all the time—except, of course, the wicked. In fact, such stories of Jesus's invariable perfection are told over and over again in the Gospel of the Infancy, where everything comes easily to Jesus, Mary, and Joseph, their powers for good are quickly recognized and rewarded, and the populace of every place they go soon comes to adore them, while the wicked stand no chance whatsoever.

Not so in the Infancy Gospel of Thomas. This collection of tales takes a strangely realistic look at the circumstances that might have arisen if a little boy had vastly more divine power than he could competently use. Some readers may be troubled to discover that, in some of the stories early in the text, when Jesus is offended he kills his opponent. When teachers try to instruct him, he publicly humiliates them; if they try to physically discipline him, he strikes them down. At first, understandably, the citizens of Nazareth are terrified of him and even demand that Joseph move his family away. They see in Jesus something demonic. But as Jesus matures he gains more control over his power. He cures those whom he injured, he proves the villagers wrong when they think a dead boy must have perished from having offended him, and he begins to volunteer to help and to save others. Gradually the villagers begin to surmise that he may be someone with the power of a divine spirit. And then they hypothesize that he might be an angel come to earth or even a God on earth. By the end of the story, Jesus has matured to the point that the final story of the boy Jesus in Thomas's gospel is the first story about the boy Jesus in the canonical Gospel of Luke, one that shows him politely teaching and learning from the elders of the Jerusalem temple.

A YOUTHFUL GOD IN A HUMAN VILLAGE

Those who read the Infancy Gospel of Thomas are sometimes appalled at the stories they find there. "Jesus could not have killed anyone," they think. "That's just preposterous!" And, of course, they are right. This is all fiction. But if we try, we can understand the point of view of the authors of the fiction. Jesus, in Christian teaching, is both entirely God and entirely human. This is a difficult enough idea when applied to a mature man, but what about somebody who is five years old? If Jesus was entirely human, then he sometimes behaved like a five-year-old, but not with the limited power of a normal five-year-old. The Infancy Gospel of Thomas was not compiled in order to show the invariable wonderfulness of Jesus. Rather, Thomas was compiled with a certain amount of realism in mind, realism that takes into account the sort of reactions children have when they feel slighted and the sort of reactions adults have to immature prodigies in their midst. The Infancy Gospel of Thomas is devoted to Jesus as a boy, and shows that he grew quickly into a wise and mature young person. It takes what appears to be the radical step of assuming that he was not born from the womb as a wise and mature person, but that he started out as a little boy and had to learn to handle his neighbors and himself carefully.

Devotion to the Infancy of Jesus

Devotion to the holy infant Jesus is not entirely lacking today. In contemporary Catholic Christendom we find particular devotion to the infant Jesus in the reverence given to the Infant of Prague, where an eighteen-inch-high statue of young Jesus, beautifully gowned and bejeweled, is said to grant the wishes of those who are devoted to him. When Prague was invaded in 1631 the statue was lost and only recovered a decade later, badly damaged, its hands ruined. At that time a priest heard the infant Jesus say, "Have pity on Me and I will have pity on you. Give Me my hands and I will give you peace. The more you honor Me, the more I will bless you." The statue was repaired and devotion to it increased to the point that statues of the Infant of Prague became common throughout the Catholic world, especially in Italy, many Spanish-speaking countries, and Catholic sections of the United States.

Replicas of the Infant of Prague are often displayed in a niche above the words "The more you honor Me, the more I will bless you." In Prague the statue has more than seventy ornate garments and it is the privilege of the Carmelite sisters of the Child Jesus in Prague to change those garments for special liturgical occasions. In Prague, Oklahoma, on Jim Thorpe Boulevard, a canonically established Catholic shrine to the Infant of Prague has been established to facilitate Americans who want to express their religious feelings through reverence of the infant Jesus. The kind of devotion that the infancy gospels display in regard to baby Jesus and baby Mary is not entirely lacking in the Christian world today.

For most Christians today, however, knowledge of the ancient stories about Jesus and Mary as children has essentially disappeared. This is something of a shame because it removes an element of mystery and amusement from the Christian religion. Perhaps the stories, as they are told here, will bring some of that back into the lives of readers.

About Titles and Texts

The names of the three ancient documents discussed in this book are all somewhat problematical. The first is known in scholarship as the Protoevangelion of James, a title added to it in later times; its original title may have been something along the lines of "Birth of Mary: Revelation of James." The word "protoevangelion" means "pre-gospel" or "early gospel" because the book covers the period from just before Mary's conception until a time just after Jesus's birth. Recently, scholars such as professor Ronald Hock of the University of Southern California, who has written an excellent study on the infancy gospels of James and Thomas, have chosen to call it simply "Gospel of James," because very few English speaking people have ever heard of a protoevangelion and because the term "gospel," thanks to the recent discoveries of the Gospel of Philip, the Gospel of Judas, the Gospel of Mary Magdalene, and so forth, is beginning to be applied to a much more diverse set of texts than just the four canonical gospels.[5] I will use the title "Gospel of James" here. No James known to us—neither the brother of Jesus nor a son of Zebedee—wrote this book.

The second document gives us a title in its first line: "The Book of Joseph the High Priest," explaining a little later that this man is Joseph

Caiaphas, a historical person who was high priest during the time of Jesus's later life and his crucifixion. Well, Joseph Caiaphas no more wrote books of legends about Jesus than he wrote *Moby Dick*, but then, James did not write the Gospel of James, just as Philip did not write the Gospel of Philip. The use of pseudonyms for the authors of ancient Christian texts was common and widespread, occuring both in the titles of canonical and noncanonical documents. It is not clear whether this document is supposedly the entire Book of Joseph the High Priest or whether only the first section of it was taken from a source by that name; all we know is that the first sentence informs us that "The Book of Joseph the High Priest, a man who lived during the time of Christ, contains the following." But how much of what follows does this imply? We do not know. Substantial portions of the text were adapted from the Gospel of James and from the Infancy Gospel of Thomas, and some were adopted from the Book of Joseph the High Priest.

Scholars refer to the text as the "Arabic Infancy Gospel" because an Arabic version was available for translation in the late seventeenth century through which the text became known in academic circles. Because that Arabic version is now lost, that translation has became our principal source. But scholars generally do not believe that it was originally written in Arabic but, more probably, that it was originally in Syriac. To call the text the "Arabic Infancy Gospel" gives the false impression that the book derives from Arabia or that it contains particularly Arabic materials, which it does not. At the end of the text we are told that it is a Gospel of the Infancy and so I will call the text the "Gospel of the Infancy" and note that it contains portions of The Book of Joseph the High Priest and significant portions of other ancient accounts as well.

For a long time the third text was called the "Gospel of Thomas." Now, however, another Gospel of Thomas, a list of 114 sayings of Jesus, has appeared in the Nag Hammadi manuscript discovery of 1945. I have published an annotation and commentary in this Skylight Illuminations series on the Gospel of Thomas that was found at Nag Hammadi.[6] It is completely and entirely unrelated to the present infancy gospel. If we want to be fair to the texts, we should call one the "Sayings Gospel of Thomas" and the other the "Infancy Gospel of Thomas." The latter usage is common today while the sayings gospel seems to have taken possession of the unmodified name "Gospel of Thomas." Along with all other modern scholars of early Christian writings, I will refer to the book of stories about the young Jesus as the "Infancy Gospel of Thomas."

For anyone seriously interested in further study of the Gospel of James or the Infancy Gospel of Thomas, I particularly recommend Ronald Hock's *The Infancy Gospels of James and Thomas,* in which the original Greek and his English translations are side by side for easy comparison and are accompanied by learned footnotes about details of the manuscripts, thereby making good versions of the original Greek texts easily available to be used.[7] Harm Smid's commentary on the Protoevangelion (the Gospel of James) offers a full discussion of many details and aspects of the original Greek text.[8] Earlier translations by William Wake,[9] Alexander Roberts and James Donaldson,[10] Montague James,[11] Edgar Hennecke, Wilhelm Schneemelcher and R. McL. Wilson,[12] B. Harris Cowper,[13] and David Dungan and David R. Cartlidge[14] were very helpful in guiding the construction of the versions of the Gospel of James, the Gospel of the Infancy, and the Infancy Gospel of Thomas in the present work. My version emphasizes the folk-tale style of these stories and is, in a way, a continuation of the telling of stories that were never intended to be solemn devotional literature but rather were supposed to be exciting and amusing tales that could be expected to change every time they were retold.

Folk Religion and Folk Literature

The infancy gospels are examples of folk literature. They originated from and then circulated among illiterate people in the form of orally transmitted stories. Eventually, of course, the stories must have been written down or they would be lost to us forever. Those who put the stories into writing generally formed them into what they thought would be a more or less coherent whole narrative, but who those authors were, and who first created the various stories, is unknown to history.

Sometimes the oral stories were just written down in no particular order, as is the case with the Gospel of the Infancy's accounts of the holy family's time in Egypt. Sometimes, though, folk literature shows a bit more sophistication, as in the case of the Infancy Gospel of Thomas, where the stories show a gradual awakening on the part of Jesus to the need for control of his divine powers and an increasing understanding on the part of the villagers of Nazareth of Jesus's special nature. We should keep in mind, however, that these are not texts wholly created by individual authors. Most of the stories embedded in the narratives circulated and were told and retold separately before and after the final author wrote them down.

Folktales about the powers and adventures of holy persons give insight into the piety of the illiterate women, men, and children who made up the populace of the Church. I believe that anyone interested in the history of early Christianity should pay particular attention to folktales like these that arise from the spirituality of ordinary people. Apart from them, we know only the ruminations, speculations, and theologizing of the elite, who are but a tiny minority in the early Church, or in any church.

Years ago I wrote a doctoral dissertation on folktales in early Christianity. Those folktales were not about Jesus, but were stories that had arisen about Jesus's earliest apostles. The stories appear in texts called the Apocryphal Acts of the Apostles and tell us about the travels, adventures, and miracles of Peter and Paul, John, Philip, and Thomas. The earliest of these accounts were written at about the same time as the earliest of the infancy gospel accounts, which is to say toward the end of the second century.

Since publishing my dissertation, I've continued to write about the earliest Christian books outside of the Bible, such as the Secret Book of John and the Sayings Gospel of Thomas, in addition to authoring books about the New Testament itself. I'm very pleased to have had the opportunity in this book to think and write about the infancy gospels. I find them fascinating and am convinced that anyone interested in the rise of Christianity should turn to both the canonical and noncanonical information we have available and pay attention both to the ideas of the literate elite and those of the illiterate masses. The ideas of the illiterate masses are best expressed through folk literature, such as the infancy gospels.

Both the infancy gospels and the Apocryphal Acts of the Apostles reveal that Christian tellers of tales assumed that the presence of the divine in the world gave certain people—the apostles and Jesus—power to do anything: to control nature, to destroy idols, and most especially to heal the sick. Their folktales are not centered on what came to be the great issues of grace and salvation. Instead, their authors used their powers of imagination to envision what might have happened when God, in the person of Jesus, traveled through the world embodying divine power. It would seem that people then, as now, daydreamed about what might happen if a God on earth came to them and helped them directly and immediately overcome their problems and their illnesses. In the absence of this happening in their immediate reality, they enjoyed imagining and then telling about what they thought could have happened during those few years when God and God's delegates supposedly walked on the earth and lived among us.

The Qur'an and the Infancy Gospels

Not only are the infancy gospels important in the development of Christian legends and for the construction of Christian heroes and heroines such as Joachim and Anne, they are also important to Muslims. Several of the stories found in infancy gospels but missing from Christian scripture appear in the Qur'an. The story of young Mary's being fed by angels is found both in the Qur'an and in the Gospel of James; the story of the baby Jesus speaking aloud the gospel about himself is found in the Gospel of the Infancy and in the Qur'an; an account of the boy Jesus making clay birds come to life is in the Infancy Gospel of Thomas and in the Qur'an.

The presence of these stories in the Qur'an reveals several significant facts. First, because Muslim tradition holds that Muhammad was illiterate, the presence of these "apocryphal" stories in the Qur'an shows that the tales circulated freely as oral traditions, as folktales that were told rather than read. Second, since Muhammad certainly heard these tales from Christians, we can be sure that Christians at his time were not as completely constrained by canonical accounts of Jesus's life as Christians are today. Indeed, Muhammad's knowledge of Jesus's life mixes canonical with noncanonical stories quite freely, and we can be confident that in this way he imitates the Christians from whom he learned the stories. Finally, it seems that the influence of such stories are preserved in the Gospel of James influenced Muhammad profoundly, to the degree that Mary is the only woman in all of the Qur'an who is mentioned by name. For Muslims, however the Qur'an is not evidence of Muhammad's knowledge and ideas but is entirely from Allah; therefore, for one billion Muslims, some of the infancy gospels' stories have the status of divine revelation.

Other Recently Discovered Gospels

Until recently the term "gospel" almost always referred to the canonical books of Matthew, Mark, Luke, and John. But in recent decades, we have been hearing about the Gnostic gospels of Philip and of Judas and Mary, the Sayings Gospel of Thomas, and others. We might wonder whether the infancy gospels are like these other new gospels. The recent discovery of new gospels means that we need to be careful to distinguish between the radically different sorts of books that are all being labeled with the same word. For example, the Gnostic gospels of Judas and of Mary, which have received so much attention in the press in recent years, are long dialogues between Jesus and favored disciples expounding in very complex and sometimes incomprehensible fashion the cosmological theories of the Gnostic Christianity. As such, they are radically different in their structure, their literary form, and the ideas they present from any of the gospels found in the Bible. The Sayings Gospel of Thomas and the Gnostic Gospel of Philip are collections of individual and isolated sayings and speculations that are not connected by any continuous narrative at all.

Thus if we think of a gospel as telling the story of Jesus in the style of a biographical narrative, which is certainly the case for the biblical gospels, none of the recently discovered gospels mentioned above would fit into that category.

The infancy gospels, while fictions drawn from the Christian folklore of a somewhat later period than the canonical gospels are, in fact, in the style of a biographical narrative. In their literary form and in their interest in telling a chronological account of events in the lives of Jesus and his family, the infancy gospels discussed in this book are more akin to the biblical gospels than any of the other "gospels" of which we know.

No one will say that the infancy stories are historically factual, and hardly anyone will argue that they are crucial to Christian belief. But they do remain interesting. They give us our greatest insights into the Christian people's religion of ancient times, not the religion of the literate elites, but the tales told by ordinary folk. I hope they continue to amaze and to amuse.

The Gospel
of James

1 Because of the *Gospel of James*, Christian legend knows Joachim, which means "Ya(weh) will establish," as the father of Mary. The *Histories of the Twelve Tribes of Israel* are fictional records that serve to give an aura of factuality to James's account. The name Joachim may derive from the short story entitled "Susanna," an addition to the Book of Daniel that is included in the Hebrew Bible apocrypha. Susanna is the wife of Joachim, who, like Mary's father, was a very rich and prominent Jewish man. Two elderly judges became passionate for Susanna, and as she was bathing in her secluded garden they crept up on her and threatened to accuse her falsely of adultery if she refused to sleep with them. She did refuse; their false witness led to her being condemned to death, but as she was being led away, Daniel interrupted the proceedings, cross-examined the elderly judges, and revealed their lies. They were soon executed. Susanna's parents, family, and husband Joachim rejoiced that she had been proven innocent, and Daniel became greatly respected.

2 There is no such law and there was no high priest named Reuben at this time. Because of his wealth and generosity, Joachim evidently assumed that he had the right to be first in line to bring his offerings.

3 Both Jewish tradition and common sense tell us that righteousness and fecundity do not go together. Nevertheless, behind the Gospel of James's statement lie the popular beliefs that children are a reward from God and that God rewards the righteous. For a counter-example, there is no implication in the Abraham story that he remained childless until he was one hundred years old (Genesis 21:5) because he lacked righteousness.

4 Fasting for "forty days and forty nights" uses an idiom found in the Hebrew Bible that means "a long time." It occurs with some frequency. For example, the flood of Noah lasted forty days and nights (Genesis 7:12); Moses spent forty days and forty nights on Mount Sinai receiving the commandments (Exodus 24:18); on the strength of a single meal Elijah traveled forty days and nights to approach God on Mount Horeb (1 Kings 19:8); and Jesus spent forty days and nights fasting in the desert following his baptism (Matthew 4:2). A forty-day fast would probably kill an elderly man.

☐ Joachim and Anne: The Gift of Mary

The Histories of the Twelve Tribes of Israel record that an extremely wealthy man named Joachim made his offerings to God in two ways. He said to himself, "I'll dedicate my great wealth to the benefit of all the people and I will also give to the Lord, hoping that my sins will be forgiven by His mercy."[1]

However, at one of the great Temple festivals in Jerusalem, where all of the people of Israel brought gifts to the Temple, when Joachim prepared to offer his gift the high priest Reuben stopped him and told him that it is against God's law for a man without any children to be the first to bring his offerings.[2]

Joachim, very worried, went off to research into the archives of Israel's twelve tribes to see if there were any other righteous men who had no children and, indeed, he discovered that every righteous Israelite had begotten children.[3]

When Joachim remembered the story of Abraham the patriarch, and how at the end of Abraham's life God gave him Isaac, he became even more depressed and he withdrew from human companionship, even from his wife. He went into the arid wilderness, set up a tent, and began to fast for forty days and forty nights. He said to himself, "I am not going to eat or to drink until I have communicated with God. Prayer will be the only eating or drinking I will do."[4]

(continued on page 5)

3

5 The name Anne reflects the influence of the story of Hannah, the mother of Samuel. Indeed, the name Anne, from the Greek "Anna," is derived from the Hebrew name "Hannah." Like Anne, Mary's mother-to-be, Samuel's mother was barren and, as the story has it, her co-wife Peninnah mocked and ridiculed her. In desperation, Hannah prayed to the Lord and God promised her a child, Samuel. In return, Hannah pledged to give that child to the Lord by giving him into service in the Temple. As Hannah is aligned with Anne, so Mary herself is aligned in this story with Samuel (1 Samuel 1–11). Significantly, Samuel is the man who inaugurates the first Kingdom of God when he anoints first Saul and then David to be kings of Israel. Mary's son will inaugurate the Kingdom of God as the Christian religion understands it.

6 There are implications of suicidal depression both in the case of Joachim and in the case of Anne. Judaism speaks of a "mitzvoth of rejoicing" or a requirement for celebration and happiness on each of the three great pilgrimage festivals to the Jerusalem Temple: Passover, Pentecost, and Tabernacles.

7 This dialogue is more realistic than most that occur in these texts. Anne's servant Judith has been critical of her, and Anne snaps back at her by implying that she may have been given the new headdress by a man trying to seduce her. While ritual impurity was contagious and could be spread by touch, moral impurity was not contagious, except in the sense that if you accepted something given for an improper action (such as knowingly receiving stolen goods), you could become a party to the action.

8 The quarrel continues; Judith's point of view reflects that of early Jewish society, indeed most of the world's premodern societies, where childbearing was thought to be a woman's fundamental purpose in life. For women, then, overcoming barrenness would be the greatest possible miracle.

Meanwhile Anne, Joachim's wife, was distressed in two ways. She said to herself, "I will go into mourning because I don't have any children and because my husband intends to die."[5]

As the time for another great Temple festival approached Anne's maid Judith said to her, "How long are you going to be so depressed? The Lord's feast is here and it is against his law to be so sorrowful.[6] Here, take my headdress, it's expertly made. It's not right for me to wear it since I'm just a servant, but you can wear it because you are a fine lady." But Anne replied, "Take it away! I'm not used to fine things like that, and besides, the Lord has humiliated me. Furthermore, I'm afraid that a seducer may have given that headdress to you and that if I take it, your sin might pollute me too."[7]

Judith said, "Why would I want more trouble to come to you? I couldn't wish for a greater curse to be on you than you already have. You are a barren woman and a mother to no one in Israel."[8]

(continued on page 7)

9 The story of Sarah is foundational to Judaism. She was Abraham's elderly wife, a barren woman in her nineties who was miraculously granted the power to bear a child (Genesis 18). She gave birth to Isaac so as to begin Abraham's lineage that God promised to make as numerous as the stars. This motif of the barren woman becoming mother of a very special child is taken up by the Christian canon, where the story of Sara and Abraham is reflected in the story of John the Baptist's parents Elizabeth and Zechariah. There again we hear of two elderly childless people who are, by a miracle, given power to have a son (Luke 1:7).

10 The idea that people will ridicule Anne within the area of the Temple is related to Hannah's story, for she was mocked by her co-wife when they went up to the Temple together (1 Samuel 1:7). Using a garden as the setting is reminiscent of the Susanna story, where the main action takes place in the private garden. In both stories, the garden signifies a private place where women can be alone.

11 This poem shows Anne feeling that she is not only rejected by her own people but also that her own nature has been betrayed. In her society the purpose of women, if not people in general, is to have children, and so for barren women life has no meaning. In terms of growth and reproduction the lives of fish and birds and the soil itself are full of meaning, but barrenness makes Anne's life seem meaningless.

Now Anne was utterly heartbroken. She washed her hair, brought out her wedding gown, put it on and at three o'clock in the afternoon walked out into her garden, where she sat beneath a laurel tree and prayed. She said, "God of my forefathers, give me your blessing and help me as you helped Sarah when, in her old age, you gave her Isaac to be her son."[9]

Anne glanced up into the laurel tree and saw a sparrow's nest. Now, even more unhappy, she said, "Oh dear, who begat me and whose womb gave me life so that I should have come to this, so that I would end up ridiculous in the sight of the people of Israel? They will even make fun of me in God's Temple![10]

What am I like?

I am not like the birds of the sky, for they have their nestlings.
What am I like?
I am not even like an animal, for the animals have babies of their own.
What am I like?
I am not even like the waters, for the waters teem with schools of fish.
What am I like?
I am not even like dirt, for dirt gives life to plants and so praises God."[11]

1 This story parallels closely the story of Samuel's mother, Hannah. In the Hebrew Bible, Hannah is elderly and barren but her prayer is answered and she conceives. After Samuel is born he stays with his mother until he is weaned, then she brings him to the Temple and tells the priest, "I give him to the Lord; I give him to the Lord for his entire life" (1 Samuel 1:27). The author of the Gospel of James seems to have in mind a parallel: just as Samuel anointed and thus created the first (Saul) and second (David) kings of Israel, so Mary gave birth to the Messiah, the final divine king. In the Qur'an 3:35–36, showing the influence of the Gospel of James, Anne says to God (about Mary, her daughter-to-be), "Thus a woman from the House of Imran said: 'My Lord, I have freely consecrated whatever is in my womb to You. Accept it from me; You are Alert, Aware!' When she gave birth, she said: 'My Lord, I have given birth to a daughter.'—God was quite aware of what she had given birth to, for a male is not like a female—'I have named her Mary, and ask You to protect her and her offspring from Satan the Outcast.'"

2 While the story in the Gospel of James is somewhat ambiguous and might be understood to be a miraculous conception, it is more likely that the miracle is that Anne is now miraculously made fertile. Accordingly, Joachim must hurry home to be with her.

3 Anne was afraid that she would be widowed due to elderly Joachim's long fasting.

Joachim is the host of what the Native American cultures of the Pacific Northwest coast called a "potlatch," where a man with accumulated wealth shows his generosity and solidifies his social standing by generously giving everything away in a great feast. Here, however, it is not implied that Joachim is left poor at the end of the feast. Joachim's great wealth, announced in the first sentence of the story, is affirmed.

4 Presumably this is stipulated because at this time the conception of Mary occurred.

☐ Mary: The Story of Her Birth

Suddenly an angel of God stood next to her and said, "Anne, Anne, God has heard your prayer and I tell you that you will indeed have a baby and that baby will some day be famous throughout the whole world!"

Anne replied, "As God lives, I declare that whatever child I bear, boy or girl, will be pledged to a life in God's service.[1]

Two more angels appeared and told Anne, "Joachim is now coming home along with his shepherds because an angel came to him too and said, "Joachim, Joachim, God has heard your prayer. You must hurry home to Anne, because she's going to have a baby!"[2]

Joachim immediately instructed his shepherds, saying, "Bring me ten unblemished lambs for sacrifice to the Lord God, ten perfect calves for the priests and elders of the Temple, and a hundred young goats to be a feast for all of the people." As Joachim and the shepherds approached, Anne stood next to the gate and watched them come and then ran up to Joachim and hugged him, crying out, "God has blessed me! I was afraid I would be a widow, but no longer; I was barren, but now I am going to have a child!"[3]

Joachim stayed home for the next day.[4]

(continued on page 11)

5 In early centuries the high priest wore what were called "*urim* and *thummim*," which may have been polished stones in the breastplate of the priest's garment or a form of sacred dice carried in the priest's garment (Exodus 28:30). The *urim* and *thummim* were used as divination devices to receive a "yes or no" answer from God. The only description of their use is in 1 Samuel 14:40–44, where Jonathan, the son of Saul, is identified as having broken a commandment of his father. In this part of the story of Mary's birth, Joachim receives a "yes" for the question of whether his sins have been forgiven by means of a form of divination, but the priest's golden circle is fictional. Scholars doubt that the *urim* and *thummim* were used by the Second Temple priesthood (520 BCE–70 CE), however, the historian Josephus writes that the high priest in the first century CE wore jewels of sardonyx that would shine brightly to give God's prophetic responses to questions.

6 The name Mary is from the Hebrew Miriam. In the Hebrew Bible Miriam is Moses and Aaron's sister and it was generally assumed that she was the woman who, when Pharaoh sought the deaths of Hebrew infants, placed baby Moses in the water to be found by Pharaoh's daughter. Therefore, as Miriam rescued Moses from Pharoah, so Mary (and Joseph), when Herod sought to kill the infants of Bethlehem, rescued Jesus from Herod by fleeing to Egypt.

In Leviticus chapter 12, instructions are given for the purification of a mother after birth. After eighty days she will go to the Temple, bringing a yearling ram and a young dove for sacrifice, in order to provide for the purification of her blood. The story implies that Mary was given milk by a wet nurse up to that time so that the impure state of her mother would not be passed on to her.

On the next day, he brought his gifts to the Temple and said to himself, "If God is going to be favorable to me, it will be obvious through divination by means of the golden circle the priest wears on his forehead." Joachim paid careful attention to that shining surface as he went toward the altar and discovered that God had forgiven him of all his sins, so he left the Temple feeling very pleased and returned to his home.[5]

Nine months later Anne gave birth to a child and asked the midwife, "Is the baby a boy or a girl?" The midwife replied, "A girl!"

Anne said, "God has strengthened my soul!" She lay in bed together with her baby. After the ceremonies of purification were past, Anne nursed the child and named her Mary.[6]

1 This story shows Mary to be precocious, walking at six months. Ordinary dirt will not make a person ritually unclean, but even so Mary is protected from it. The point of the story is not to convey plot or character but to prove by narrative that Mary remained pure in all senses of the word. The reader can understand from this report that Mary was raised in a wealthy family where rugs covered all the floors.

2 The pure women are, presumably, under the age of twelve and so free from any risk of the perfectly acceptable and normal ritual impurity that menstruation and sexual activity bring about. Mary will be raised strictly kosher and nothing by way of food or persons that might be ritually impure will be allowed into her sacred space. She is being kept away from all possible sources of pollution. While she is still nursing, her mother constructs a holy and ritually pure space for her; after that she will take up residence in the holiest place on earth, the Temple in Jerusalem.

3 Mary's father repeats Anne's pledge to give Mary to Temple service; this echoes the installation of Samuel in the Temple more than 1,000 years earlier. In that story his mother, Hannah, pledges her son into Temple service.

The priests' unqualified blessing and acceptance of Mary contrasts with the story of Jesus's rejection and trial. It is almost the polar opposite of the Passion narrative, for here the priests affirm Mary in front of all the people. Historically speaking, since no woman had any part to play in Temple sacrificial services, it is impossible to imagine what role the priests are supposed to have had in mind for little Mary. Note that it is not her accomplishments, at the age of one, but her essence, her being, that they are praising. The priests and "all the people" seem to be miraculously aware of Mary's future role as the mother of the Messiah.

☐ Mary: Raised in Blessing and Purity

The baby grew stronger every day so that by the time she was six months old her mother stood her up on the ground to see if she was able to walk. She walked seven steps and ended up back in her mother's arms. Anne picked her up and declared to her, "As God lives, you won't walk on the ground again until you walk in the Temple of the Lord."[1]

Anne made her bedroom a sacred place and forbade anything common or ritually unclean to come near it. She invited several pure women of Israelite heritage to help raise Mary.[2]

When Mary was one-year-old her father Joachim celebrated by hosting a feast, and the priests and the scribes, the elders, and all the people of Israel were invited to come. Then, when all were assembled, Joachim formally offered the girl to the Temple priests. They blessed Mary, saying, "Bless this girl, God of our fathers, make her fame last throughout all generations."

All the people replied together, "Let it be so."

Then, a second time, Joachim pledged Mary to the priests for Temple service and they responded, "Bless her, most high God, with blessing forever."[3]

(continued on page 15)

4 The fictional high priest Reuben was the one who, earlier in the story, told Joachim he could not make his offering first because he had no children. Anne's song occurs in the same narrative place as the song of Hannah, mother of Samuel. Her song is a hymn praising the powers of God (1 Samuel 2:1–10) and rejoicing that God has saved her (from a life of barrenness). Similarly, Zechariah, the father of John the Baptist, sings a triumphal song at the birth of his son (Luke 1:68–79). Mary herself praises the powers of God in reference to the prospective birth of Jesus in the "Magnificat" (Luke 1:46–55), a song named for its first word (in Latin), "*Magnificat anima mea Dominum*," or "My soul magnifies the Lord."

5 This section of the story may possibly reflect practices in pagan cults where sacred virgins were kept carefully separated from the ordinary people. For example, in Roman religion the "vestal virgins," who were priests of Vesta, the goddess of the hearth, were sometimes enrolled for training as early as age three. Women in Judaism, even ritually pure Jewish women, were not permitted into the Temple beyond a particular "courtyard of the women." Ritually pure Jewish men could enter one courtyard further, the priests further still into the area of the Temple altar, but the high priest alone could go into the small Temple enclosure called the Holy of Holies, and then only on Yom Kippur, the day of atonement.

6 The story continues to assume that Mary's family and the Jewish priestly establishment are aware of Mary's future role as the mother of God incarnate. The author of the Gospel of James may have in mind the fact that the Hebrew name Yehoshua, which is also written as "Joshua" and as "Jesus," means "God saves." The fact that Mariology, particular Christian devotion to Mary, is assumed here and elsewhere is evidence for the relatively late date of James's gospel.

Anne picked Mary up and nursed her, singing this song to God:

"This is a new song I sing to God
He visited me and removed my shame
He gave me the benefit of his righteousness
Tell the sons of Reuben the Priest that Anne nurses her
    baby!"[4]

Anne brought Mary back to the consecrated bedroom and then went out and helped with the feast. After it was over, everyone left praising Israel's God.

When Mary was two years old Joachim suggested to Anne, "Let's take Mary to the Lord's Temple in Jerusalem so that we can complete our pledge to God; if we don't He might become angry and refuse to accept our gifts."

Anne, however, replied, "No, let's give Mary another year at home so that she won't miss her mother and father quite so much." Joachim agreed.

When Mary was three years old Joachim said, "Bring the Hebrew women who are pure and tell them to carry their lamps lighted and lead Mary into God's temple. She needs to stay there to make sure that she doesn't turn away from the Lord."[5]

The women led Mary in and the priest greeted her there with a blessing and a kiss. He said, "God has blessed you in every generation and in the end, thanks to you, God will save Israel's people."[6]

(continued on page 17)

7 This is a particularly pretty passage. Mary is shown to be comfortable and happy making a new home in the Temple. Her parents leave her and disappear from the story, never to be mentioned again.

Mary dances before God as David did and is fed by angels, so we know that the absolute purity of her food and her life is beyond question. The Qur'an knows this legend and assumes, like the Gospel of James does later on, that the high priest in Jerusalem is named Zechariah. The Qur'an (3:36–37) says that God accepted Mary graciously and "caused her to grow like a lovely plant, and told Zechariah to take care of her. Every time Zechariah entered the shrine to see her, he found she had already been supplied with food. He said: 'Mary, how can this be meant for you?' She said: 'It comes from God, for God provides for anyone He wishes without any reckoning.'"

The Christians from whom Muhammad learned Christianity believed wholeheartedly in the stories written in the Gospel of James.

Mary sat down on the altar's third step and God gave her grace; she danced on her feet in the Temple and everyone in Israel loved her. Her parents went home thanking and praising God, because their daughter was content and did not try to follow them. From that time on, an angel brought Mary's food to her and Mary lived in God's Temple, as carefully cared for as if she were a dove.[7]

1 The Gospel of James, which has tracked Mary's age rather carefully from her birth, to her mother's purification, to her walking at six months, and to her entry into the Temple at age three, now reports a crisis because whether it would be possible for a little girl to reside in the Jerusalem Temple (it would not be); certainly a menstruating young woman could not possibly dwell there. Menstruation inherently produces impurity, and impurity, if brought into contact with holy things, would profane them and anger God (Leviticus 15:19–24) Impurity is a purely ritual category, a normal and morally neutral state that can be transmitted and must be taken into account especially in connection with holy things.

2 The garment with the twelve bells may be a remembrance of the high priests' garment that was emblazoned with the twelve oracular jewels known, as the *urim* and *thummim*. Or perhaps it recalls the bells that decorated the lower hem of the high priest's garment (Exodus 28:33). By the time the Gospel of James was written, the Temple had been destroyed for a century and details of its functioning were no longer known to ordinary people.

3 Zechariah here is the high priest, although there was no historical high priest by this name at that time. In the Gospel of Luke, Zechariah, the father of John the Baptist, is a low-ranking priest who only occasionally serves in the Temple.

The assembly of widowers introduces the idea that Joseph is an elderly man. While an elderly Joseph is part of Christian art and lore until the present day, in the canonical gospels of Matthew and of Luke he appears to be a young man preparing for his first marriage and there is no mention of any "widower" status.

□ Joseph: Mary's Protector

When Mary turned twelve, the Temple's priests began to worry and they met together wondering, "If she's turned twelve, won't she begin to pollute the Lord's sanctuary? What can we do?"[1]

They turned to the high priest and said, "When you are at the high altar of the Lord, be sure to go into the very holiest place and ask God about Mary. Whatever God reveals to you, that's what we'll do." The high priest donned his ceremonial coat with twelve bells attached and entered into the Holy of Holies to ask God what should be done about Mary, now that she was about to become a woman.[2]

An angel appeared there and said, "Zechariah, collect all of the widowers in Israel and tell each one of them to bring his walking stick. God will choose one of them by a special sign and he will become Mary's husband," and so Zechariah sent out messengers who ran to every part of Judea. God's trumpet rang out and all of Israel's widowers assembled together in Jerusalem.[3]

(continued on page 21)

4 In the ancient world and among human beings generally, unusual occurrences are taken to be signs, oracles, and portents. Zechariah was expecting a sign, but what the sign would be he does not seem to know in advance. Josephus, a Jewish historian from the first century, lists several signs that he thinks were given by God as a sign of the Temple's coming destruction in 70 CE. These included portents taking place in the Temple itself: a cow giving birth to a lamb; the huge brass inner court gate opening at midnight all by itself; and priests in the inner court hearing a mystical voice saying, "We are departing from here."

The symbolism of a dove as a sign from God occurs in the story of Jesus's baptism where the Holy Spirit descends in the form of a dove. The story of the men using sticks to seek an oracular sign as to which of them would take charge of Mary is mentioned in the Qur'an; translators differ on a key word indicating slim pieces of wood: for some it is "reeds," for some "arrows," for others "pens." In T. B. Irving's version of the Qur'an (3:42–46), we read that "the angels said: 'Mary, God has selected you and purified you. He has selected you over all the women in the Universe. Mary, devote yourself to your Lord; fall down on your knees and bow alongside those who so bow down.' Such is some information about the Unseen we have revealed to you. You were not in their presence as they cast lots with their pens to see which of them would be entrusted with Mary. You were not in their presence while they were so disputing. Thus the angels said: 'Mary, God announces word to you about someone whose name will be Christ Jesus, the son of Mary, who is well regarded in this world and the Hereafter, and one of those drawn near to God. He will speak to people while still an infant and as an adult, and will be an honorable person.' She said: 'My Lord, how can I have a child while no human being has ever touched me?' He said: 'That is how God creates anything He wishes. Whenever He decides upon some matter, He merely tells it: 'Be!', and it is.'" Again, the Gospel of James has influenced the Qur'an's story of Jesus's mother. In another passage (19:16–34), the Qur'an tells the story of Jesus's birth from the virgin Mary due to God's miraculous decree. The Qur'an's story includes the angel's annunciation to the virgin Mary, but Joseph plays no role at all.

When he heard the high priest Zechariah's request, Joseph dropped his ax and joined the widowers, who were hurrying to the Temple bringing their walking sticks. The high priest took each man's stick, entered the Temple, and prayed to God, but God did not give him any special sign. When Zechariah came back out he returned the walking sticks to their owners. Joseph was the last one to get his back and, as he took his stick from the priest, a dove flew out of it and perched on him! The priest told Joseph that this miraculous sign certainly meant that he had been chosen by God to care for Mary.[4]

(continued on page 23)

5 The Gospel of Mark (6:1–6) and the other canonical gospels mention Jesus's brothers by name (James, Joseph, Judas, Simon) and note that he had sisters as well. Paul calls James, whom he has met personally (Galatians 1:19), "the brother of the Lord." However, because later Christian tradition affirmed Mary's perpetual virginity, the necessity arose to understand biblical reports about Jesus's siblings as something other than full brothers and sisters, fellow children of Mary and Joseph. They were regarded commonly as step-siblings or cousins. In the Gospel of James, this process of redefinition begins and Jesus's siblings are now understood to be step-brothers, children of the widower Joseph and his late unnamed wife.

6 These men are mentioned in Numbers 16:1–40; they, along with many others, challenged Moses's leadership and sought to assume priestly roles without divine permission. God punished them by fire and earthquake. The passage in Numbers concludes with the admonition that no one other than a priest in the lineage of Aaron may offer incense to the Lord.

Joseph said that he wouldn't do it. "I'm old" he said, "and I already have sons of my own. Mary is just a little girl and I'll be laughed at if I take her."**5**

The priest replied, "Hear the Lord God! Remember what God did to Dathan and Abiram and Korah. They disobeyed him and were destroyed when the earth opened up and they dropped down into it forever."**6**

(continued on page 25)

7 Joseph will protect and take care of Mary, but he will never be her husband in this gospel's story. This creates a problem for him later in the narrative, when he does not know how to classify Mary for taxation purposes. The Gospel of James makes every effort to prove that Mary's virginity was not in any way compromised by the elderly widower Joseph. He is not her husband in any sense, and after he assumes responsibility for her, he leaves her behind as he pursues his work. In the timing of the story, Mary is just twelve years old and prior to her first menstruation, since she has just left the Temple precincts.

The only thing we know about Joseph's trade from the gospel tradition is that Jesus in Mark 6:3 and Joseph in the corresponding passage in Matthew 13:55 are said to be *tektons*, skilled workers and builders of houses, a position we might call a general contractor. A *tekton* might have done work as a mason, a bricklayer, a roofer, a carpenter, or all of these at once. Since houses in Galilee were usually made of stones, a builder of houses wouldn't primarily be working in wood. A *tekton* from the little village of Nazareth almost certainly would primarily have been employed in the construction of the city of Sepphoris, only an hour's walk away. In the narrative in the Gospel of James, however, Joseph is a Jerusalem-based housing contractor and presumably a reasonably well-to-do man.

Fearful, Joseph agreed to protect and take care of Mary. He turned to her and said, "I'll take you out of God's Temple and I'll have you stay in my own house. I'm going off now to build some houses, but I will be back. Meanwhile God will take care of you."[7]

(*continued on page 27*)

8 There was no "tribe of David," unless by this is meant the tribe of Judah, from which David came. The author intends readers to understand that Mary is descended from the royalty of Judea, for David was the founder of the royal lineage; "tribe of David" here means "house of David," or "descended from David." The Mishnah, a third-century book of Jewish law, custom, and practice, says that eighty-two young girls were responsible for weaving the veil of the Temple (Shekalim 8:5).

The veil of the Temple, first described in Exodus 26:31, was a gorgeous tapestry of astral symbolism that separated the Temple's Holy of Holies from the surrounding holy places. The ancient historian Josephus (who was, in his early life, a priest in the first century CE Temple) wrote that the veil with which he was familiar was embroidered with many colors, including scarlet, blue, and purple, and that it contained images of the universal elements of fire, earth, air, and sea, each denoted by a particular color, while the whole of the veil represented a mystical vision of the heavens.

9 These colors are among those mentioned in Exodus and by Josephus. To the Christians reading the Gospel of James, scarlet would have hinted at the blood of Christ; purple meant royalty in Roman times, just as it does now.

10 With this reference, the author of the Gospel of James shows that he and his audience were familiar with the story of John the Baptist's birth found in the first chapter of the Gospel of Luke. It is odd that the birth story of a rival first-century Jewish religious cult leader would be given at all in the birth story of Jesus, but Luke does so; it is odder still that this story would be extended and elaborated the way it is here in the Gospel of James. Zechariah was not high priest nor was anyone named Samuel in the first century. The point of this sentence in the Gospel of James is to correlate its narrative time sequence with the time sequence in Luke's gospel.

The priests in the Jerusalem Temple met together and decided that it was time to make a new Temple veil. The high priest said, "Bring seven virgin women from the tribe of David," and his servants brought them together in God's Temple. The high priest told them to be sure to include Mary.[8]

When they were assembled he told them, "Cast lots among yourselves and determine which of you will spin the golden thread, the blue thread, the white, the scarlet, the purple, the fine linen and the silk." Her lot indicated that Mary should spin the scarlet and the purple into thread, so she picked up those materials and went home.[9]

This happened at the time when the high priest Zechariah was struck dumb in the Temple and Samuel replaced him until he was again able to speak.[10]

1 There is no well mentioned in the canonical scriptures. However, today in Nazareth there is a source of water going back at least to the first century that is called "Mary's Well." It is not a deep, excavated well but a water supply brought in from a nearby spring. Throughout the history of Christian iconography, the annunciation scene takes place at a well or a fountain of water, thanks to the account written here.

2 These words of annunciation are from Luke's gospel, but there the first sentence is spoken by an angel (1:28) and the second by Elizabeth (1:42). Here the voice is of an angel, but unlike the canonical angel whom Mary saw, this angel is invisible.

3 Note how the author, at this crucial point, focuses our attention by giving the reader precise details of Mary's actions.

4 The miraculous conception of Jesus is the subject of the first element of Mary's question. The second element, about how the child will be born, foreshadows a theme that occurs later in the Gospel of James, that Jesus's birth was not natural because Mary remained a physical virgin even after giving birth.

5 These passages are a development from Luke's gospel (1:34). The author of the Gospel of James is being very careful to make it clear that Jesus's birth is a miracle and that no human male was involved. Further, the author intends to make it clear that because God caused Mary to conceive, it follows that Jesus is God's Son, which is a line of thought that is not explicitly spelled out in the canonical gospels. Today, most Christians now take it for granted that since Mary conceived miraculously, Jesus was God's Son. The Qur'an, by contrast, affirms the divine and miraculous conception of Jesus to the virgin Mary, but insists that the conclusion that Jesus is therefore God's son is incorrect (Qur'an 19:35).

6 This statement is taken from Matthew's gospel where it is addressed to Joseph, not to Mary. The literal meaning of Jesus, "YHWH saves," is the background for the sentence.

☐ Mary: Miraculous Conception

Mary took the scarlet and purple material and began to spin it into thread. Later that day, she took a pot and went out to draw water from the nearby well.[1]

A voice spoke to her saying, "Hail, you who are most favored, the Lord is with you. Blessed are you among women."[2]

Mary looked to her right, and her left, and all around, but saw no one and so, trembling, she went back into her house, put down her water pot, and sat down and began again to spin her purple thread.[3]

Suddenly an angel stood next to her and said, "Don't be afraid, Mary, for the God of everything favors you." She wondered what that might possibly mean. And the angel continued, "The Lord is with you. You will conceive by God's word!"

Mary was puzzled and replied, "Do you mean that I will conceive from the living God and that my child will be born in the natural way?"[4]

"No, Mary," said the angel. "The power of God will come over you and therefore the holy child you will bear will be called the Son of the Most High God.[5] Because he will save his people from their sins you will name him Jesus."[6]

(continued on page 31)

7 As the story is being told here, this is the moment of conception. Mary is, in the story's chronology so far, just twelve years old.

8 In Luke's gospel Mary is said to travel from Nazareth in Galilee to the hill country of Judea in order to visit Elizabeth. This would have been a long and arduous trip, and an unaccompanied young woman would not have been able to travel so far. In the Gospel of James, however, Mary lives in or near Jerusalem and Elizabeth, it turns out later in the narrative, lives in Bethlehem, which is six miles from Jerusalem, and so the trip is not an unreasonable one.

9 Elizabeth is John the Baptist's mother, as we learn from Luke's gospel. The pregnant Elizabeth cannot be working on material for the Temple veil because, according to the story, only virgins were permitted to do so. How Elizabeth knows Mary is "my Lord's mother" is not given, but we are entitled to guess that it was divinely revealed to her. It is interesting to note here that the baby John the Baptist has blessed Mary from within Elizabeth's womb.

10 While the canonical account is almost always direct speech, the Gospel of James frequently tells readers the internal thoughts and moods of its main characters. Here, somewhat surprisingly, we learn that Mary has temporarily forgotten what she was told by Gabriel and so does not understand why she is specially favored. Perhaps she didn't understand the angel; her questions earlier in the narrative show that she is unclear as to what the angel is talking about. This is the first time in this story that we have heard the angel's name: Gabriel.

11 Mary's age is a problem in the transmission of the Gospel of James. By the reckoning of the story itself, which has been carefully monitoring her age throughout, she is twelve at this point, and some manuscripts have that as her age. But even in ancient times, this was an early age for a woman to have a child, and so some manuscripts advance her age to fourteen, while even more give her age at this point as sixteen. In our culture even sixteen seems rather young, but our culture is the exception in world history. In most ancient cultures a sixteen-year-old mother would have been nothing out of the ordinary.

Mary replied, "I am God's servant, so let it happen to me just as you've said."**7**

When Mary finished spinning the scarlet and the purple thread she took it to the high priest, who blessed her and said, "Mary, God has given you fame and you will be blessed in all times to come."

Overjoyed, Mary went to the home of her cousin Elizabeth, knocked on her door, and waited.**8**

When Elizabeth heard, she dropped the bright red thread she had been working on, ran to the door, opened it, and blessed Mary, saying, "Why is my Lord's mother coming here to me? As soon as I heard you arrive, the baby inside of me leaped up and then it blessed you."**9**

Mary, who was not thinking of the mystery the angel Gabriel had told her, looked to the heavens and asked the Lord, "Who am I to be blessed for all time?"**10**

She stayed with Elizabeth for three months and she grew bigger every day. Mary began to be afraid, though, and left to return to her own house, withdrawing from public contact. She was sixteen when these extraordinary things happened.**11**

1 Joseph rather egocentrically takes Mary's condition to be an affront to his own honor. He does not blame Mary herself but assumes that some seductive man must be responsible, a man akin to the serpent in the story found in Genesis chapter 3. While Adam is not present in the Genesis story during the seduction of Eve, the notion that he was off praising the Lord is added here from folk tradition. In earlier Christian tradition theologians were prone to blame Eve for the fall rather than Adam, but in later centuries theologians spoke of the "fall of Adam" to the point that Eve's involvement began to seem secondary. Christian tradition identifies Christ as a new Adam and Mary as a new Eve, emphasizing that in both cases the new persons do not repeat the sins of the original persons. Here, ironically, Joseph takes Mary to be a new Eve who does repeat the sin of the original.

2 It is inconceivable that a girl could really have been raised in the Holy of Holies, but the emphasis put on this point in the Gospel of James would have encouraged readers to think of Mary as akin to the Ark of the Covenant. The Holy of Holies was originally constructed to house the Ark. The Qur'an (3:37) emphasizes the miraculous provision of food to Mary in the sacred place when it says that God miraculously provided food for Mary in the Temple's sanctuary. Unlike the canonical gospels in which Jesus predicts the Temple's destruction (e.g., Mark 13:1–2), the Gospel of James consistently takes a very positive and uncritical view of the Temple and of the Jewish priesthood.

3 Note how clearly this text insists that Mary has never slept with a man. While the canonical accounts in Matthew's gospel has long been understood to imply this, it does not actually say so, and some scholars, such as Jane Schaberg and Robert Miller, are convinced that the canonical evangelist did not intend to imply what he did not say, for he does not specify the supposedly central point that Mary was miraculously impregnated without male involvement. Rather, those scholars argue, the canonical gospel describes Mary's pregnancy as being caused by a man's impregnating her and that the Holy Spirit affirmed that this impregnation was in accordance with the will of God.

☐ Joseph and Mary: Accused and Tested

During Mary's sixth month of pregnancy, Joseph returned from his trip to build houses outside of Jerusalem. When he arrived, he discovered that the virgin had grown very visibly pregnant and he slapped himself in the face, fell to the ground, and said, "How can I possibly look to the Lord God and whatever can I say about this young woman? I took her in as a virgin directly from the Temple of God and I have obviously failed to preserve her virginity! Who deceived me? Who did this wicked thing in my own house, seducing and defiling the virgin?

"This is the same thing that happened to Adam; he was in the Garden off by himself praising the Lord when along came a serpent who encountered Eve alone and seduced her. Now the same thing's happened to me."[1]

Joseph got up from the ground, called Mary, and said, "You were so very much favored by God, why have you done this? Why have you disgraced yourself? You were brought up in the very Holy of Holies at the Temple! Angels fed you!"[2]

Mary, crying, replied, "No, I haven't done anything wrong. I never have slept with a man."[3]

"So," Joseph said, "how can you explain the fact that you're pregnant?"

(continued on page 35)

4 | It is odd that in this gospel's story, Mary has forgotten Gabriel's message to her both here and in her earlier conversation with Elizabeth. Evidently the author wants to portray Mary's internal thoughts and concerns with some realism rather than portray Mary, as later traditions do, to be someone who instantly understands all that is implied by her condition. In the Gospel of James, Mary's understanding evolves. Her whole experience, according to James's gospel, is of a voice and then a brief discussion with an angel. The words "the power of God will come over you" sound as if something will physically happen, but in this account the angel's annunciation declares what will happen and then the angel departs. No other event takes place, and so, except for that one brief encounter, Mary would not have a clue why her pregnancy occurred unless, as in the canonical gospels, she has a supernatural level of comprehension.

5 | Again we have an internal monologue whereby readers share Joseph's thoughts. In the ancient, world unusual occurrences were often understood to be miracles, and so Joseph wonders if Mary might be telling the truth and, if so, he imagines that she might have been impregnated by an angel. It is not clear what law might account for Mary's being threatened with execution; she is not engaged or married to Joseph. If he gives responsibility for her over to somebody else, then he might well face disgrace, but there are no legal grounds for her to be killed. The reasonable thing for him to have done would be to return Mary into the care of her parents, but this option is not explored and so, as their advanced age was stressed in the earlier narrative, the reader will assume that they have died.

6 | This passage begins with a close approximation of the story, as told in Matthew's gospel (1:20–25), but without Matthew's emphasis on a fulfillment of prophecy or Matthew's concluding lines about Joseph taking Mary to be his wife. In the Gospel of James, he resumes his guardianship over Mary with the implication that he will not be leaving her alone again. In James's gospel Mary and Joseph never marry nor are they ever engaged to be married.

"As God lives," Mary said, "I don't know how it happened!"[4]

Joseph, frightened, left her alone, saying to himself, "If I try and cover up her crime, I'll be guilty myself of breaking God's law. But if I make her condition public, then I'm risking the execution of someone who might possibly be innocent. Perhaps her baby does come from an angel. What can I do? I think I'll just quietly make her go away."[5]

Night fell and Joseph was asleep when, in a dream, an angel came to him saying, "Don't be afraid to keep that young woman with you because, I tell you, the baby inside her is from the Holy Spirit. She is going to have a son and you will name him Jesus because he will save his people from their sins." Joseph woke up and praised Israel's God for giving him such a privilege. Then he watched carefully over Mary from that time on.[6]

(continued on page 37)

7 The high priest in the Jerusalem Temple from 6 CE to 15 CE was named Annas. His daughter was the wife of Joseph Ciaphas, who was high priest at the time of Jesus's crucifixion. However, we know nothing of a scribe named Annas.

8 A secret marriage would not have been a possibility in this culture, but the prospect seems to be derived from Annas's desire to give Joseph the benefit of the doubt. Note that Joseph was entrusted with Mary to maintain her virginity and so even a legally permissible sexual relationship is a crisis in the world created by this narrative.

9 This is the third time the narrative has mentioned that Mary received food from angels, so it must have been an important point to the author of the Gospel of James. Mary's hearing angels singing has not been mentioned before, but perhaps it was implied by her dancing in the Temple; David dancing before the ark may be in mind here. That Mary is raised in the Holy of Holies, hearing angels, dancing before God and eating angelic food, is a grand scenario and implies a unique closeness between the celestial and earthly Temples in the person of Mary. This prefigures her elevation in rank, within Catholicism, to Queen of Heaven.

A scribe named Annas came to Joseph and asked him, "Where have you been? We haven't seen you since you came back home."**7**

Joseph replied, "I was tired out after the trip and rested here in the house."

Annas looked around and spied the very obviously pregnant Virgin Mary. He left the house, ran to the high priest, and told him, "Joseph whom you trusted so much has committed a heinous crime; he was entrusted with a virgin and he has defiled her. He took her from God's holy Temple and now he's married her secretly, telling nobody about it."**8**

The high priest responded, "Joseph? Has he really?"

Annas replied, "If you'll send servants over to Joseph's house, they'll see that she's pregnant."

So the high priest sent servants and they saw that the situation was just as Annas said it was. Both Joseph and Mary were bound over for trial.

As their trial began, the high priest asked Mary, "What have you done? Why have you forgotten God and debased yourself, and how can you have forgotten that you were raised in the Holy of Holies at God's Temple? You even took your food from angels and heard the angels singing! You danced before God! Now, why have you done this thing?"**9**

Mary began to cry, but she answered, "As God lives, He knows I am innocent and that I have never had sexual relations with a man."

The high priest turned to Joseph and said, "Why did you do this?"

Joseph replied, "As my God lives, I have not had relations with her."

The high priest responded, "Don't lie. Tell me the truth, you married her secretly, didn't you, and you kept it quiet from the people of Israel? You haven't humbled yourself to obey God so that He will bless your children." Joseph said nothing.

(continued on page 39)

10 Many cultures have what are called "ordeals" that provide legal evidence in cases where evidence doesn't exist. "Dunking" a witch into water to see if she would sink (and show innocence) or float (and show guilt) is a relatively well-known medieval ordeal. Here the theory is that if Joseph drinks the bitter water and survives and returns from the hills, he will be proven innocent. There is nothing in Hebrew Bible law or later Jewish law that prescribes such an ordeal for a man suspected of violating a virgin woman.

11 The only trial by ordeal found in the Hebrew Bible appears in Numbers 5:11–31 and it provides the background for the curious story here in the Gospel of James. The book of Numbers describes an ordeal in considerable detail that is designed to determine whether a woman whose husband suspects her of adultery is innocent or guilty. The details of the ordeal process include a procedure where a priest gives "bitter water" to the woman under suspicion to drink. The priest prepares the bitter water by taking holy water from the Temple's supply and adding some dust from the Temple's floor, dust that would have been in contact with the holy blood of sacrifices. Finally he washes ink into the bitter water from a written curse that he had previously spoken aloud to the woman. He then burns the written curse on the altar, after which the woman drinks the bitter water. If she were guilty, it was expected that she would swell up and die. There is nothing in the book of Numbers about the suspected woman being sent into the desert, but it makes the story in James more dramatic.

12 The ordeal is understood to be divine revelation and thus God confirms Joseph and Mary's testimony to their innocence. Here, as often in its narrative, the Gospel of James assumes that the whole population of Jerusalem is intensely interested in Mary's situation and status.

The high priest said to Joseph, "Surrender the virgin you received from God's Temple," and Joseph wept. The high priest continued, "I decree that you both must undergo the ordeal of God's bitter water, which will expose your lies publicly." The high priest prepared the bitter water and Joseph drank it, then Joseph was led out to a place in the hills.[10]

When Joseph returned, he was entirely healthy! Next, Mary drank the bitter water and went into the desert hills, but she too returned in perfect health.[11]

Everyone was amazed that Joseph and Mary were not found guilty. Then the high priest said to them, "Since God hasn't exposed your sins, I can't condemn you." He sent Mary and Joseph away from the Temple and Joseph took Mary home to his house, rejoicing and praising God.[12]

1 As Luke's gospel tells the story, Joseph and Mary had to go to Bethlehem for a taxation census and, in Bethlehem, Jesus was born. In the Gospel of James's account, oddly enough, only people from Bethlehem have to be accounted for, while in Luke's account all men have to return to their native villages. Historians point out that there never was a time when people had to return to their ancestral villages to be registered for tax purposes and that the only census of the period was that of governor Quirinius, which took place around 6 CE, a good ten years after Jesus was born, for Jesus was born during the reign of king Herod, and Herod died around 4 BCE. The idea of a taxation census is borrowed from Luke. Both Luke and Matthew believe that prophecy (Micah 5:2) requires that the Messiah be born in Bethlehem, and that since Jesus is the Messiah, he must have been born in Bethlehem. Since he is Jesus of Nazareth in Galilee, both authors must explain how a birth in Bethlehem in Judea could have been possible; the construction of a story about the taxation census is Luke's method.

2 The Gospel of James never mentions Joseph having daughters, although according to Mark's and Matthew's gospels, Jesus did have sisters. Joseph's sons account for Jesus's brothers in a way that allows for Mary's perpetual virginity.

3 Joseph's internal monologue reaches no conclusion. The author of James's gospel tends to show his characters' thinking as confused and sometimes forgetful or flawed, which makes his story more interesting and realistic than sacred narratives in which the central figures are invariably perfect. Here Joseph does not know how to categorize his committed relationship with a pregnant unmarried woman of marriageable age to whom he is not related. If Joseph claims Mary as his wife, by the standards of the narrative he will be shamed because he promised to leave her a virgin and not to take her as a wife. Joseph is Mary's third guardian in a few years: she spent three years with her parents Joachim and Anne, then she was "adopted" by the Temple priesthood, and after she turned twelve she became a ward of Joseph. We can see why the question of her standing under taxation law would be a difficult one!

☐ Mary and Joseph: The Christmas Story

A decree came from the Emperor Augustus ordering everyone from Bethlehem in Judea to be listed for purposes of taxation.[1]

Joseph said to himself, "I'll certainly make sure that my own sons are listed, but what about this girl Mary?[2]

Should I list her as my wife? But that will shame me. I can't list her as my daughter because everyone knows she isn't my daughter. Well, I'll let the Lord's will happen when the time comes."[3]

(continued on page 43)

4 Jerusalem is only five or six miles from Bethlehem, and so this journey would take only a couple of hours. A walk from Nazareth to Bethlehem would take several days.

5 The marker for three miles to Bethlehem would put them just about
halfway on their short journey. Much of the rest of this passage is
obscure, but possibly it has a connection with the idea that some people will receive salvation through the birth of Christ and other people
will not. As Jesus put it, there will be a separation between the sheep
and the goats. Note that the narrative is now taking place from
Joseph's point of view. Earlier, for example during the time when Mary
stayed with Elizabeth, the narrative adopted Mary's point of view. The
author, adopting the guise of the omniscient narrator, sometimes gives
us the thoughts of Mary, sometimes those of Joseph.

6 This is the Gospel of James's Christmas scene: a cave in the desert
just about halfway between Jerusalem and Bethlehem, an outdoor
setting in the arid Judean wilderness. The historical date of Jesus's
birth is not known, but if it were in the period December through Feb-
ruary, the weather might have been rather cold and snowy, although
unlikely, it would have been a possibility. We can sympathize with
Joseph's eagerness to find an experienced woman to help out when his
young pregnant ward is about to go into labor.

Mary is left alone in the cave; Joseph's sons stand guard outside
while Joseph goes toward Bethlehem, which cannot be very far away.
The gospels give three different versions of the journey to Jesus's birthplace. For Matthew, the holy family already lives in Bethlehem and only
later journeys to Nazareth. For Luke they live in Nazareth and, to reg-
ister for taxation, journey to Bethlehem where Jesus is born. Here, in
the Gospel of James, they journey from their home in Jerusalem toward
Bethlehem but do not enter it. In historical fact, Jesus was probably
born in Nazareth and not near Bethlehem at all; the story of his being
born in Bethlehem was constructed on the assumption that he must
have fulfilled a prophecy found in Micah 5:2, one that originated more
than 700 years before Jesus was born.

He saddled his donkey and Mary rode on it out of Jerusalem as Joseph and his sons walked close behind.[4]

They were coming near Bethlehem and were at the marker for three miles when Joseph noticed that Mary was very unhappy, so he said to himself, "Maybe the baby is painful to her," but when he looked again she was laughing happily. He asked her, "Mary, how is it that sometimes you appear so sad and other times all happy and joyful?"

Mary replied, "I see two kinds of people, some are sad and mournful, the others happy and full of laughter."[5]

As they began again to ride further toward Bethlehem, Mary said to Joseph, "Take me down from the donkey. I can feel my baby struggling to be born."

Joseph replied, "But we are surrounded by desert here."

Again Mary said, "Help me down, for the baby is struggling even harder."

Joseph took her down from the donkey and said, "But where can I take you so that you can have some privacy?" Noticing a nearby cave, he helped Mary into it and told his two sons to guard the entrance while he himself went on toward Bethlehem to find a Hebrew midwife.[6]

(continued on page 45)

7 This may be the most poetically beautiful passage in all of early Christian writing. Rather than announce the birth of Jesus, the author of James's gospel uses indirection so that the reader must infer that he is just then being born. As Joseph walks toward Bethlehem, time suddenly stops. Nothing special happens, he sees no angels, hears no heavenly trumpets, but he notices that time has ceased to flow, and he notices this by seeing very common sights—workmen eating, goats drinking, and so forth. The sudden cessation of time signifies the end of the initial stage of humanity and the beginning of humanity's final stage. Jesus said, about this change in the nature of time, that "The Law and the Prophets were proclaimed until John; since that time the Gospel of the kingdom of God has been preached, and everyone is forcing his way into it" (Luke 16:16). The Western world has acknowledged the change in time by naming the present era's years "anno domini," each a successive year of the Lord dating, in theory, back to the precise moment described here in the Gospel of James: the moment of Jesus's birth.

The narrative here shifts into the grammatical first person and Joseph speaks to the reader directly of his experience. In Luke's Acts of the Apostles we see a similar technique, for Luke occasionally shifts from the usual third person to first person, and suddenly instead of "they went here, they did that," we learn that "we went here and we did that." Acts 21:1–18 is one example of Luke's technique.

8 It seems odd that Joseph and the midwife in a place only three or so miles from Jerusalem are said to be so careful to signify their Hebrew status. Perhaps Mary's purity would be threatened by the services of a ritually unclean gentile midwife. Implicitly the customs and procedures of a Hebrew midwife will be somewhat different than those of a gentile midwife, and she and Joseph want to be sure that they share the same cultural expectations.

As I, Joseph, walked toward Bethlehem and I ceased to be moving, looking up into the sky I saw the astonished clouds come to a halt, the sun no longer moving, birds stopped in mid-flight. I looked down again and saw workmen near the road seeming to eat their lunch. Some had their hands on the dish, some lifted food toward their mouths but they did not move, some had their hands lifted toward their heads, but their hands were immobile while their faces were uplifted. I saw sheep on the nearby hills, none of them moving, all stood perfectly still. A shepherd had raised his hand to swat at one of them, but his hand remained frozen in place. When I looked toward the stream there were goats with mouths open in the water about to drink from it, but they did not drink for they were still. Then, suddenly, motion began again.[7]

I noticed a woman coming down from the hills, who came up to me and asked me, "Where are you going?"

"I'm heading into Bethlehem to find a Hebrew midwife."

"Are you a man of Israel?" she asked.

"Yes, I replied."[8]

"Where is the woman who is about to give birth?"

(continued on page 47)

9 In assuming Mary is yet to give birth, Joseph fails to understand the implications of his recent experience of time's cessation. Until this point in the narrative Joseph has avoided the implication that he and Mary were in any way planning to be married, but here the same Greek word is used as in Luke 2:5, *emnesteumene,* meaning betrothed or engaged to be married.

10 We can almost hear the skeptical tone of the midwife's question here; and readers of the modern text need to bear in mind that in the ancient world, virtually everyone who ever heard the Gospel of James heard it read aloud and enacted. Most literate people, who were few in number, read aloud even when reading by themselves.

Here in the narrative we have a plot summary for readers (or, better, hearers) who may have forgotten the earlier parts of the story or who came in late.

11 The brilliant cloud of light signifies the birth of a God and is the counterpart to the star of Bethlehem in the heavens. The idea of the birth of Jesus coming to pass through blinding light may relate to the idea in the Gospel of John that Jesus is divine light (John 1:4–5, 8:12). Since Jesus literally means "God saves" and the Christian religion preaches Jesus as the savior, the midwife's declaration is an ironic identification of the arrival of Jesus with the arrival of salvation before she knows his name.

I answered, "In that cave back along the road. She is my fiancée.⁹

"She's not your wife?" the midwife asked.

Joseph replied, "Her name is Mary. She was raised in the Holy of Holies, in God's Temple, and by sacred chance she came to be under my protection, but she is not my wife. She conceived through the Holy Spirit."

"Is that so?" asked the midwife.

"Come along and see," said Joseph.¹⁰

Accompanied by the midwife, Joseph returned to the cave where a cloud of brilliant light shone from inside. "Today my soul is strengthened," said the midwife, "for I've seen incredible things! Salvation has come to Israel!"¹¹

(continued on page 49)

12 This is the poetry of light joining the earlier poetry of time. What is going on in the cave is far beyond human comprehension; but nevertheless, it is what Mary has been prepared for her entire life. If she, raised in the Holy of Holies, is akin to the ark of the covenant, then the light blazing forth here is akin to the spectacle of the ark's cover opened. To this day, Christmas carols feature the motif of extraordinary light at Jesus's birth. For example, the carol "Silent Night" sings of the "Son of God, love's pure light, radiant beams from thy holy face, with the dawn of redeeming grace Christ the Savior is born." The Gospel of James wants to create the impression that Jesus was not born in the natural manner but that he appeared first as pure light and then as a nursing baby. Jesus's birth needs no assistance from a midwife; God alone implements Jesus's birth.

13 In the New Testament, Salome, whose name is from the Hebrew "shalom" or "peace," is the name of one of Jesus's followers. She is one of the three women who was present at the crucifixion and who visited Jesus's tomb Easter morning. In Matthew's gospel her name is not used, but there we are told that "the mother of the sons of Zebedee" was present; perhaps she and Salome were the same person. Salome in the Sayings Gospel of Thomas's saying 61, declares herself to be a disciple of Jesus.

14 Testing Mary's continued virginity after the birth of Jesus is a delicate issue, but it is straightforwardly dealt with in the narrative. It seems odd that there should be a professional midwife present and yet another character would do the testing; maybe we have a combination of two narrative traditions here. The scene is reminiscent of the story of doubting Thomas in the Gospel of John. There Thomas will not accept the idea of Jesus's resurrection unless he can see the scars of the nails in Jesus's hands, put his finger into those scars, and put his hand into the wound in Jesus's side. Jesus subsequently appears and invites Thomas to do so, at which point Thomas declares Jesus "my Lord and my God" (John 20:24–29).

At that instant, the brilliant cloud moved out of the cave; inside, even more intense light illuminated everything so brightly that they could hardly stand it. Little by little the light dimmed, until they glimpsed a newborn baby and then they saw him nursing at Mary's breast.[12]

The midwife shouted, "What a wonderful day! I'm so glad to have seen these glorious sights!" She left the cave and Salome met her at the cave's entrance. The midwife told Salome, "I've just seen the most awesome sight. A virgin gave birth, which is wholly unnatural."[13]

Salome said to her, "As the Lord lives, if I don't get proof of this claim I am certainly not going to believe that a virgin had a baby."

Salome entered the cave and said, "Mary, let me examine you. You've caused quite a controversy." Salome tested Mary with her hand and found the midwife's claim confirmed, for Mary was proven still to be a virgin.[14]

But immediately Salome's hand withered up painfully, as if burned crisp in a fire, and she screamed, "Oh no, because I didn't believe I have tempted God. Now my hand is flaming and about to drop off!" She begged God, saying, "God of my fathers, remember that I am a descendant of Abraham, Isaac, and Jacob. Don't humiliate me but let me return to my parents in good health. You know that I've lived a good charitable life, done good works in your name, and up to now you have rewarded me."

(continued on page 51)

15 As in later legends, many of which are found in the Gospel of the Infancy, Jesus is treated in the narrative as a kind of glowing, supernatural magic object. By his very physical nature miracles occur. The baby is a piece of divinity, a glowing object from a different world, a world of light and of healing power.

16 Here Jesus is portrayed as a "king" whom people come to worship instead of a "god" worthy of worship. In the ancient world of the Mediterranean, as in the ancient worlds of the Maya, the Egyptians, and the Chinese, kings were categorized as gods or at least as primary mediators with gods. Accordingly, the emperor of Rome was sometimes declared to be a god and the king of Judea to be a son of God (Psalm 2:7). The idea of Jesus as incarnate God and as legitimate ruling king would have gone together more smoothly in those days than now.

At that moment an angel appeared beside Salome and told her, "God has heard you and all you need to do is reach over to the baby, touch him, and your hand will be healed."[15]

Joyful, Salome went over to the baby and said, "I'll certainly touch him," and she intended to worship him, saying, "He is a king born to Israel."[16]

Immediately, she was entirely healed and a voice came to her: "Say nothing of the strange things you have seen today until the child comes to Jerusalem." Salome left the cave, and God approved of her.

1 It is curious that people find it so easy to imagine following a star to a particular destination. Just try it! A star might, at best, point to a particular direction at a particular period of the nighttime, but simple observation will reveal that stars move across the sky all night.

In the Gospel of James at this point we have the theme of gentiles in the persons of magi coming to Jesus informed, it appears, by the wisdom of their own religion and not of Judaism. The idea is borrowed from the Gospel of Matthew's story of the magi. The magi from the east were professional astrologers and magicians, and in some cases priests of the Zoroastrian religion where rituals focused on the purifying power of fire were common. Their homeland is today called Iran, and it has also been called Persia; during Jesus's time and the time of the Gospel of James, it was known as Parthia.

2 This is a reference to Micah 5:2, a passage that probably originates from a parallel drawn between Bethlehem being David's hometown at the very dawn of the Judean royal lineage and thus the speculation that Bethlehem would be the Messiah's hometown when that anointed king arrives. Accordingly, it's particularly odd that the Gospel of James pointedly places Jesus's birth in a cave outside Bethlehem, in contrast both to Matthew's and Luke's gospels, in which he is born in that town.

3 It seems as if only the magi could see the star. Herod certainly didn't see it. The idea that Persian magi would be interested in using their astrology to determine the birthplaces of Judean kings in order to come worship them is borrowed from Matthew's gospel. If we understand the star to be the celestial light that accompanies Jesus and surrounds the cave of his birth, then considerable time has passed since he was born, so as to allow the magi time to discover the light, analyze it, make their journey, and then to arrive near Bethlehem. Perhaps they could see ahead of time the light that became visible at the moment of Jesus's birth.

☐ The Magi: In Search of a King

Soon Joseph prepared to move into Judea, for Bethlehem had become chaotic after the arrival of magi from the east who were asking, "Where is the new Judean king? We saw his star in the east and we've come here to worship him."[1]

Herod, hearing about this, was quite upset and sent some of his servants to the magi to question them. Also, he sent for priests and asked, "What do the scriptures say about the Christ's birthplace?"

They replied, "The scriptures say that it will be Bethlehem of Judea."[2]

He told them to leave. He turned to the magi and asked them, "What have you seen to indicate that a new king has been born?"

They replied, "We saw a huge star so bright that it washed out the light from all other stars until they became invisible. That told us that a new king of Israel had been born and we journeyed here in order to worship him."[3]

Herod said, "Go find him and, when you do, let me know because I want to go and worship him too."

(continued on page 55)

4 The star of Bethlehem in the Gospel of James's account seems to be more like an angel than a phenomenon of the night sky, and there's no indication that it can be seen by anyone but the magi. Here the ancient science of astrology seems to be combined with ancient idea of angelic guidance. The metaphors of light found in the Gospel of John have become real events in the Gospel of James.

5 There are no historical records of any attempt by Herod to murder the children of Bethlehem. The story was invented by Matthew, in part, to construct a parallel between the early life of Jesus and the early life of Moses and in part to provide a motive for the holy family to enter Egypt, so that they might upon leaving Egypt, fulfill a prophecy. The story of Moses begins with an order by Pharaoh to kill baby Hebrew boys (Exodus 1:22), but Moses's mother hides him and later places him into the marshy river side where he is rescued by Pharaoh's daughter. Similarly, Herod (in the role of Pharaoh) orders that the boys of Bethlehem be put to death, Jesus's mother hides him at first, and then the holy family flees into Egypt.

Matthew's story requires that the holy family flee to Egypt, so that they might return from Egypt to fulfill the prophecy: "Out of Egypt I will call my son," (Matthew 2:15, Hosea 11:1). In the book Hosea, the "son" is a metaphor for the people of Israel, called out of Egypt during the exodus. For Matthew to regard the Hosea passage as a prophecy about Jesus, the holy family must be in Egypt so that Jesus can be called out of it, and because there must be a reason for them to be there, Herod's persecution is constructed as a narrative device to provide that reason.

6 For this part of the story, the Gospel of James is following the Gospel of Matthew quite closely, but with a few differences. Here the famous line from Luke's gospel (2:12), where an angel tells the shepherds that they will find a baby wrapped in swaddling cloths and lying in a manger, describes Mary's attempt to hide Jesus from Herod's minions.

The magi left and the star that had gone before them continued on, leading them all the way to the cave and into it, until it stopped right above the baby Jesus.**4**

When the magi saw the baby there with his mother Mary, they brought out gold, frankincense, and myrrh and offered it to him.

An angel warned them not to go into Judea, so they returned to their homeland a different way.

When Herod discovered that the magi had disobeyed him, he flew into a rage and sent men to murder every little child of Bethlehem, the two-year-old children and every baby younger than that.**5**

Mary, terrified that her son might be killed, took her baby and wrapped him in swaddling cloths and laid him in the manger.**6**

1 The Gospel of James ends the story of Mary, Jesus, and Joseph right here, with no evident interest in tracing the family into Egypt. The remainder of its narrative features the story of baby John the Baptist, his parents, and that family's persecution by Herod. Presumably this account, like the discussion of the events surrounding John's birth that are given in the Gospel of Luke 1:5–80, are revisions of birth narratives told by John's own followers in the years after his death. It is very difficult to imagine why followers of Jesus would have gone to the trouble of creating birth stories about a personage who had only minor importance in their own religion.

2 From this report we have to conclude that John the Baptist, like Jesus, was born in or near Bethlehem, because Herod threatened only Bethlehem's children. Accordingly, when Mary went to visit Elizabeth earlier in the narrative, she must have gone to Bethlehem.

As light blazed from the cave where Jesus was born, so light fills the interior of the mountain where John and Elizabeth are hiding. As a star helped the magi find Jesus, a mountain now gives help to John. Nature is on the side of the sacred babies while royal authority tries to hunt them down.

3 It is hard to account for this tale being invented by Christians interested in telling the story of Jesus Christ's birth, for in their opinion Jesus was supposed to be the king of Israel. More likely, it was created by partisans of John the Baptist who believed that their own hero was the Christ. The Judean priest and historian Josephus wrote that King Herod was afraid that John might use his substantial influence over the common people to organize a rebellion. Therefore Herod brought about John's death to prevent this from happening. During the first century CE and into the second, John's followers were rivals of Jesus's followers. Their influence waned, of course, but even in this century, in the marshlands of Iraq, the Mandaean people trace their religious foundation back to John the Baptist.

☐ Herod: The Murder of Zechariah

Meanwhile, Elizabeth, hearing that murderous men were coming to kill her son John, took him out and fled into the Judean hills looking for a place to hide him, but she couldn't find a secure secret place.[1]

She felt terrified and said, "Please, mountain of God, hide this mother and her child," but Elizabeth could not climb up any further. Finally the mountain was broken in two and took them in and light blazed within it as an angel of God arrived to protect them.[2]

Herod still sought baby John, even sending servants into the Temple while Zechariah was serving as priest. They asked him, "Where is your son hidden?" Zechariah replied, "I'm working now as a priest at the altar of God! How would I know where he is?"

Herod's servants returned and told him what had happened and he was enraged, saying "Isn't it likely that his son is supposed to be the king of Israel?"[3]

Again he sent his people to Zechariah to say, "Tell us truthfully where your son is or face execution." Zechariah replied, "I'm prepared to be a martyr but, if I lose my life my spirit will go to be with the Lord while you will have the guilt of killing an innocent man in the court of the Temple of God."

(continued on page 59)

4 | The death of Zechariah reported here may have some literary relationship to the death of a prophet Zechariah mentioned by Jesus who said, "Therefore also said the wisdom of God, I will send unto them prophets and apostles; and some of them they shall kill and persecute; that the blood of all the prophets, which was shed from the foundation of the world, may be required of this generation; from the blood of Abel unto the blood of Zechariah, who perished between the altar and the sanctuary: yea, I say unto you, it shall be required of this generation" (Luke 11:49–51). Since the death of the prophet Zechariah occurs toward the end of the last book of the Hebrew Bible's histories, Second Chronicles, it is the report of a prophet's death furthest separated in time from the murder of Abel by Cain, so "From Abel to Zechariah" is shorthand for all murders of all divine messengers. Zechariah's death (2 Chronicles 24:20–21) took place in the court of the Temple, but the location is not more precisely specified. The "avenger" mentioned in the Gospel of James would have been Jesus Christ in the mind of the Christian author of James's gospel, but perhaps the avenger would have been Zechariah's son John in the minds of John's followers, or even God, whose imminent arrival on earth John predicted.

5 | The Temple itself mourns Zechariah's death. Note here the antagonism between the righteous priesthood and the wicked Herod, which is quite unlike the canonical gospels' accounts that portray the priests and the allies of Herod as allied together against Jesus. According to pilgrim reports, Zechariah's blood was still visible even up to 333 CE and quite possibly thereafter. The story of Zechariah's disappearing body, with the assumption that it was taken up by God, would remind Christian readers of the story of Mary's body, miraculously "assumed" into heaven after her death. In the Gospel of Luke, Zechariah is not portrayed as a great righteous hero, as here, but as a somewhat foolish country priest who doubts the word of an angel and therefore is struck dumb while on temporary duty at the Temple (Luke 1:20).

Then at dawn Zechariah was murdered between the Temple's entrance and the altar itself. The people of Israel were not aware of his death and so when the time for the customary salutation between priests came, the other priests went into the Temple to meet Zechariah and have him bless them. They waited a long time, but he did not appear. Finally, for Zechariah continued to be absent, one priest walked toward the holy area of the altar, where he saw dry blood crusted on the ground. A voice rang out from heaven, "Zechariah has been murdered. His blood must remain until his avenger comes."[4]

When the priest heard this voice, he was terrified and ran to tell the other priests what he had seen and heard. They returned to the altar with him and they too saw what he had seen.

The Temple itself howled and the priests ripped their own clothes apart from top to bottom. Zechariah's body had completely disappeared except for some dried blood that was hard as stone.[5]

(continued on page 61)

6 │ In this account "all the people of Israel" are on the side of the murdered Zechariah and so are in opposition to King Herod. Similarly, earlier in the Gospel of James, all of the people recognized the special
divine mission given to Mary.

The name Simeon is borrowed from the Gospel of Luke where an
elderly man, Simeon, encounters Mary and Jesus in the Jerusalem Temple. Luke describes Simeon as a devout and righteous man upon whom
the Holy Spirit rested, but Luke does not say that Simeon is a priest,
much less the High Priest. Here the Gospel of James concludes its narrative with a direct reference, a segue as it were, into the canonical
gospel story as told in Luke, for there we do hear an account of the
time that Simeon did finally see Christ arrive (Luke 2:25–35).

7 │ It is hard to know which "James" the author claims to be. If he is
James, brother of the Lord, and so Jesus's brother James, he wouldn't
have been more than two or three years old at the time of Herod's
death in 4 BCE. Similarly it could not be James, son of Zebedee, a disciple who was Jesus's contemporary. Scholars agree that the author or
authors of the book are unknown to history.

The frightened priests left to tell the people that Zechariah had been murdered. All the people of Israel heard the story, and sorrowed and mourned for three days. The priests, three days after the murder, needing a replacement for Zechariah, met together, cast lots, and found that the choice was Simeon. The Holy Spirit had promised Simeon that he would not die until he saw Christ arrive.[6]

I am James and I wrote this history in Jerusalem but, when trouble arose at the time of Herod's death, I retreated to the desert hills until Jerusalem became calm again. I praise God, who gave me the ability and the wisdom to write this history. Grace be given to everyone who fears the Lord to whom be glory throughout all time. Amen.[7]

The Gospel of
the Infancy

1 Joseph Caiaphas was, in fact, the name of the ruling high priest from 18 to 37 CE during the ministry of Jesus, including the time of Jesus's crucifixion. Joseph Caiaphas was a powerful and successful man able to work both with Temple authorities and with the ruling Roman occupying governors. There is no surviving book by Joseph Caiaphas, and if he wrote one, it would not have contained the stories in this collection of Christian legends.

2 This is a pious introduction to the whole of the narrative. A similar story about the infant Jesus preaching occurs in the Qur'an 19:30. There Jesus speaks as a baby in the cradle: "He said: 'I am God's servant. He has given me the Book and made me a prophet. He has made me blessed wherever I may be, and commissioned me to pray and pay the welfare tax so long as I live and to act considerate toward my mother. He has not made me domineering, hard to get along with. Peace be on the day I was born, and the day I shall die and the day I am raised to life again!'" And so in the Qur'an and evidently also in the Gospel of the Infancy, Jesus gives a quick summary of Christian doctrine. There is nothing in the Islamic account that a Christian would find unacceptable. The Muslim practice to this day is to say "peace be upon him" when saying the name of Jesus or any other of God's prophets.

3 The Alexandrian age began in the year 336 BCE with the coronation of Alexander the Great as king of Macedonia. Therefore, the three hundred and ninth year of that age would be 27 BCE, which is the first year of the reign of the Emperor Augustus of Rome. While Jesus's birth date is not known for sure, the canonical gospel records indicate that he was born before the death of King Herod (4 BCE), which would place the event around 6 BCE. Augustus did not issue the decree mentioned here; it is a mistaken idea that the author borrowed from the Gospel of Luke.

☐ A Cave, Not a Stable: The Nativity Story

The Book of Joseph the High Priest, a man who lived during the time of Christ, contains the following. It is said that Joseph the high priest is Joseph Caiaphas.[1]

He wrote that the infant Jesus, lying in his cradle, said to his mother Mary: "I am Jesus the Son of God and the Word of God and you have given me birth just as the angel Gabriel told you. My Father sent me for the salvation of all the earth."[2]

In the three hundred and ninth year of the Alexandrian age, the Roman emperor Augustus decreed that each man must go to his native town to be listed for taxation purposes.[3]

(*continued on page 67*)

4 | The Gospel of the Infancy, like Luke's gospel, assumes that Joseph and Mary live in Nazareth and must journey to Jerusalem and then toward Bethlehem. But otherwise, the account follows the version in the Gospel of James rather than that of Luke or Matthew because Jesus's birthplace is located in a cave outside of Jerusalem.

5 | The story of Salome testing Mary is missing here, but the remainder is a rewording of James's Gospel. The last line shows a kind of equation of Jesus and Mary that indicates an advanced Mariology, moving in the direction of an understanding of Mary as the female counterpart to Jesus.

6 | This story derives from the conclusion of the Salome story in James's gospel. The power of Jesus works without any conscious effort on the part of the holy infant. He is a location of the divine in the profane world, and the divine works through him automatically and sacramentally. Conscious intentionality is irrelevant.

We might be reminded of the woman who was healed by touching Jesus's garment (Mark 5:27–34). She was healed by power that flowed from him through his garment. Jesus did not consciously act and had to ask "Who touched my garment?" when he noticed power flow out of him. The infancy gospels assume that the baby Jesus possessed divine potency by his very nature and that during healing, a power flowed out of him. Interestingly, the story is now being told from the point of view of the old woman.

Obediently, Joseph got up and took his wife Mary to Jerusalem and then beyond to Bethlehem so that he, along with the rest of his family, might be listed in Bethlehem. But outside of Bethlehem, almost at sunset, Mary told Joseph that she was about to go into labor and that she couldn't delay in order to enter Bethlehem. So, when they came to a cave, she said, "Let's go in here."[4]

Joseph hurried away to find a woman to assist in the birth and as he rushed off he met an old Hebrew woman from Jerusalem who was walking toward the cave. He said, "Please, come to this cave and help us, for there is a woman who is going into labor."

Time passed, and it was well after sunset when the old woman, accompanied by Joseph, entered into the cave. They were amazed to discover that it was filled with lights that were more lovely than the lights of oil lamps or of candles and they seemed to be even brighter than the sun itself. They found a child wrapped in a blanket nursing at the breast of Lady Mary. Astounded at the mysterious light, the old woman asked Mary, "Are you the child's mother?" Mary said that she was and the old woman told her, "You aren't like other women." Mary replied, "My son is unequaled among children and I'm unequaled among women."[5]

The old woman told Mary, "Mistress, I hope you will reward me; I've had palsy for a long time." Mary said, "Touch the baby," and when the woman did so, instantly she was cured and she went out of the cave saying, "I am the servant of this child for the rest of my life."[6]

(continued on page 69)

7 This is a lovely vision. In keeping with trends of Christian and Jewish thought found, for example, in the canonical Letter to the Hebrews, the author envisions a time when the Temple of the heavens and worship on the earth come together as one. Christian apocalyptic hope is that this union takes place when Christ returns and the heavenly Jerusalem descends to earth (Revelation 21:2–3): "And I John saw the holy city, new Jerusalem, coming down from God out of heaven, prepared as a bride adorned for her husband. And I heard a great voice out of heaven saying, 'Behold, the tabernacle of God is with men, and he will dwell with them, and they shall be his people, and God himself shall be with them, and be their God.'" In this infancy gospel, that vision of Jesus as the tabernacle of God descending into the world is prefigured in the scene at the time of Jesus's birth. The cave has become the Temple, the tabernacle containing the presence of God on earth.

Shepherds came to the cave, and having lit a campfire outside, were happily relaxing when the skies filled with a host of angels glorifying and praising God. The shepherds too began to praise God aloud so that the vicinity of the cave became like the Temple of God in Heaven, since both in the Temple above and here below heavenly and earthly voices glorified God aloud because of the birth of Christ the Lord. The old woman, having seen these miracles at first hand, praised God, saying, "I thank you Lord God of Israel for letting me see the Savior's birth."[7]

1 This is certainly an odd story. The idea that the unnamed woman in Luke's gospel who anointed Jesus was sinful Mary Magdalene is a later legend and not in the canonical gospels. This story answers the question: What would it take to make oil sacred enough so that someone could use it to anoint the Messiah (the "anointed one") himself?

□ A Sinful Mary and the Anointing of Christ

Eight days later came the required rite of circumcision and the baby was circumcised inside the cave in accordance with God's law. The old woman took the foreskin and placed it in an alabaster container of oil of nard and gave it to her son, who sold perfumes and ointments. She said to him, "Be sure not to sell this container even if somebody offers you three hundred denarii for it." That is the same alabaster jar of perfume that sinful Mary used to anoint the head and feet of our Lord Jesus Christ and it is this same nard that she wiped from his feet with her own hair.[1]

1   A firstborn male child formally belonged to the Lord and so belonged to the Lord's Temple, as spelled out in Exodus 13:2, 12–13. A family was required, therefore, to redeem their first son through a ceremony in the Temple. It is because the son is holy before the Lord, and so at first he belonged to the Lord and not to the family, that he must be redeemed and brought into the family. He does not become "holy before God" because of the ceremony of redemption but, rather, that ceremony takes place because of the holy status into which he was born.

2   The vision of Jesus blazing like a pillar of light is a lovely one, reminiscent of the passage in John's gospel where Jesus says to Nathaniel: "You shall see the heavens opened, and the angels of God ascending and descending upon the Son of Man" (John 1:51). Simeon sees Jesus as a vision of the heavenly Temple in *the* arms of Mary. The idea of Jesus as the incarnation of the heavenly Temple is a main motif of the Letter to the Hebrews in the New Testament.

In the version of this story found in Luke's gospel, Simeon addresses first God and then Mary. Here he addresses baby Jesus directly.

☐ Jesus in the Temple

Ten days later they brought him into Jerusalem. Forty days after he was born, he was taken into the Temple and placed before the Lord and sacrifices were offered for him according to God's commandment in the books of Moses that reads, "Every newborn boy will be called holy before God."[1]

It was then that Simeon, an elderly man, saw the baby Jesus in Mary's arms blazing like a pillar of light while angels singing praise surrounded him as royal guardians surround a king. Simeon walked quickly up to Mary, stretched out his arms, and said to Christ, "Lord, let me, your servant, now leave life peacefully. I have seen the mercy that you have prepared for everyone everywhere, a light to the nations, a glory to your own Israelite people." Hannah too was there; she was a prophetess who approached Jesus and Mary, praising God and declaring Mary to be blessed.[2]

1 | Zartosht is a Persian name that usually appears in English as Zoroaster; he is the founder and prophet of the Zoroastrian religion. The magi must be coming from Persia, today called Iran, where Zoroastrianism was centered. Zoroaster taught a religion with one God, Ahura Mazda, and focused attention on the human struggle to follow the righteous path of Ahura Mazda rather than the path of chaos and evil that the demonic figure Ahriman encouraged people to follow.

2 | In this narrative the star of Bethlehem has become an angel at the service of Zoroastrian magi. The mobility of the star and its ability to rest in or above the cave wherein Jesus was born, which is part of the Gospel of James's narrative, anticipates this evolution from star into angel.

3 | Outsiders often conclude that the Zoroastrian religion is "fire worship" but, in fact, their sacred fires represent spiritual purity and moral righteousness, and so while fire can represent the God Ahura Mazda, the fire is not God and Zoroastrians do not worship fire. It is interesting that these Zoroastrian magi are assumed to understand the divine nature of the infant Jesus, just as they are said to come to worship him in the Gospel of Matthew.

☐ The Magi and Herod: Varying Views of Jesus

When Jesus was born in Bethlehem of Judea in Herod's time, magi came to Jerusalem from the east according to Zartosht's prophecy. They brought offerings of gold, frankincense, and myrrh, which they gave to the baby Jesus, for they revered him. Mary took one of his baby blankets and gave it to the magi as a gift instead of giving them only a blessing, and they accepted it as a fine gift indeed.[1]

Soon the same angel that had appeared before them as a star guiding them to baby Jesus returned and led them as a supernatural light all the way back to their own land.[2]

When they arrived, the princes and the kings of their country came to them asking what they'd done and where they'd gone and how their journey forth and back had been. They showed off the blanket that Mary had given them and in its honor they all gave a great feast. Then, because it was their national custom, they built a fire and worshipped the fire.[3]

Finally, at the climax of their ceremony they threw Jesus's blanket into their sacred fire, where it disappeared completely. Later, when the fire was extinguished, they recovered Jesus's blanket and it was not the least bit scorched. The fire hadn't touched it. They took it out and kissed it, laying it over their eyes and on their heads, saying, "It's amazing that the fire didn't burn this blanket in the least." Eventually they put the blanket into the vault where they kept their greatest treasures, doing so with the utmost respect.

Herod, when he realized that the magi from the east were never going to come back to his palace, assembled his own priests and said, "Tell me where this Christ is supposed to be born?" "Bethlehem of Judea," they replied, and Herod began to plot Jesus's death.

1 This is a transitional summary, allowing the narrative to move from the Bethlehem region into Egypt, where much of the remainder of the account takes place. All John the Baptist material is now gone from the story. At this point, we begin to go into the new narrative story of the Gospel of the Infancy. The parts before this have been interesting revisions of the story that developed from Matthew's and Luke's gospels through the Gospel of James.

The actual distance of a journey from Bethlehem to inhabited areas in the Egyptian Nile delta would be about two hundred miles. The need to flee quickly and the details about how arduous the journey was are given to add dramatic impact.

2 Soon we will see that one of the principal themes of the Gospel of the Infancy is Jesus's power to annihilate by his very presence any other demonic or supernatural potency that exists in his vicinity. While Egyptian religion was not monotheistic, some of the gods were superior to others and here the narrative specifies that the holy family encounters one of the most powerful of all of them.

3 This is, in fact, how many oracles worked in the ancient world. Priests or priestesses in ancient temples would become possessed by the deity of the temple and speak in the voice of the deity. The message the deity conveyed would then be related to any interested parties. A major Egyptian god's words would certainly be widely circulated. It is clear that the priests had considerable power to originate and to interpret those words before they left the temples.

☐ Into Egypt:
The Holy Family in Flight

It was then that an angel of God came to Joseph and told him, "Go, take the child and his mother and go into Egypt immediately, as soon as you hear the cock crow for the dawn," and Joseph got up and prepared to depart, and as he was about to begin the journey the sun rose. It was a long journey, and the saddle of the donkey wore out and broke.[1]

Eventually, they arrived at a great Egyptian city, one housing the statue of an important Egyptian god to which many subordinate Egyptian gods and idols brought gifts and made promises.[2]

A priest of this Egyptian statue stood next to it and whenever the voice of Satan came out of that idol he repeated whatever Satan had said to messengers who relayed the words throughout Egypt and even to lands nearby.[3]

That priest had a three-year-old son, and the boy suffered from possession by several devils who spoke weird things through him. When he was possessed, he'd tear apart his clothes and walk around naked, throwing stones at anyone nearby.

(continued on page 79)

4 | It is particularly interesting that the narrative uses the voice of the great Egyptian god to give evidence for Jesus's presence and his divine nature. This is reminiscent of the demons who, in the canonical gospels and especially in the Gospel of Mark, correctly identify who Jesus is even though the human beings who are present do not know. In the ancient world the exclusivist monotheism of later Western religion was not yet in place, and so while people believed their particular deity might be the most powerful, this did not lead them simply to deny the existence of others. Rather, people would bring the world of the supernatural into court, so to speak, and have other gods give testimony to the excellence of their own God.

5 | More than one thousand years before the Gospel of the Infancy came into being, the same kind of tale told here about baby Jesus was told about the Ark of the Covenant. We read in 1 Samuel 5:1–5 that the sacred ark of the Israelites was stolen by Philistines, who brought it into the temple of their god Dagon. When they returned to that temple the next morning, Dagon's priests discovered the statue of their god fallen face down in front of the ark with its head and hands cut off. Only the stump of the statue remained upright. This Israelite story would convince the Israelites who heard it that the God of Israel was much stronger than the Philistines' Dagon.

6 | Jesus's cloths are diapers, but that doesn't seem to be quite the right term to use, because it would make passages not meant to be humorous seem humorous. The proximity of cloth to Jesus's body makes it holy and powerful. The contagion of holiness is ideologically similar to the contagion of impurity. If an impure person touches something pure, it can become impure. If a holy person, ideally Jesus but even a saint during his or her lifetime, wears a piece of clothing, that clothing contracts the holiness of the person and contains some of the power of the holy person. To this day the Roman Catholic church classifies a piece of cloth that has touched the body of a saint as a "second class relic" and affirms that it contains special power.

A hostel dedicated to the Egyptian god stood adjacent to the temple of the idol and Joseph and Mary came to it and entered. The citizens of the city were frightened and therefore their leaders and priests ran to the statue and asked it, "Why is the land agitated and trembling?" The idol replied, "A God has arrived secretly, a true God. There is no other God worthy of worship; he is the Son of God and when he arrived in our country our land quaked and shook with fear. We ourselves are terrified of his immense power."[4]

Just then, at that very time, the great idol crashed down to the ground and, when they learned of its collapse, everyone in the area, all of the Egyptians, and others as well, ran away.[5]

When the priest's son, as usual, fell into a state of demonic possession, he went into the hostel and found Joseph and Mary, for only they remained after the rest of the people had run off. Mary had washed Jesus's cloths and put them out to dry. The possessed boy took one down and draped it over his head and soon devils came swarming out of his mouth and flew away from him taking the form of snakes and crows and, from that time on, the boy was well, healed by the Lord Christ's power.[6]

(continued on page 81)

Note the plurality of demons fleeing the boy. From early Christian times, when Jesus is said to have cast a "legion" of demons from a man in Gedara (which demons fled into a herd of pigs and then into the sea of Galilee), and when Saint Anthony of the desert was famously plagued by a whole variety of differently shaped demonic beings, demons were thought to travel in packs, rather than always individually, to possess particular people. Here the boy was freed from a variety of evil creatures.

7 This is an interesting view of the prophecy (Hosea 11:1) that caused Matthew to develop the story of the holy family exiled into Egypt in the first place. In Matthew the prophecy has to do with God's Son (originally the Israelite people, but to Matthew it is Jesus) being called out of Egypt and so the holy family is said to have gone to Egypt and to have returned. In this version, it is the manifestation of Jesus's power that fulfills the prophecy. The purpose of Jesus's exercise of power is to demonstrate his incarnation as the Son of God and, therefore, his possession of greater power than any of the gods of Egypt have.

He thanked the Lord who healed him. When the boy's father saw him healthy and free of demonic possession, he asked him, "Son, how did this happen, what cured you?" His son replied, "When the devils took me over, I entered the hostel and a lovely woman with a baby boy was there. I took down one of the cloths that she had just finished washing and put it over my head and instantly devils raced out of me and flew off." The boy's father was very happy and said, "Son, perhaps this baby is the Son of God, maker of heaven and earth! Just as soon as he and his family arrived here our great statue was thrown to the earth and all the other idols and gods were destroyed by power from on high." And so the prophecy that reads, "Out of Egypt I will call my Son," was fulfilled.[7]

. . . . .

1 Although in the Gospel of Mark (9:17–29) Jesus casts out a "deaf and dumb" demon, the Gospel of the Infancy has a different view of demonic power than that found in the canonical gospels. There demonic power derives from nonhuman powers, the demons, who have their own agenda, their own kingdom, and their own motivations. In this narrative, however, demonic powers are often assumed to be under human sorcerers' or witches' control. From both perspectives a sickness or a physical disability is caused by demonic force, but here the demonic force is malevolently controlled by other human beings.

2 We need to bear in mind that the demonic possessions, sorcery spells, assaults by magical snakes, and so forth found in this narrative represent the common and ordinary medical theory of that time. In the absence of anything like modern medical theory or practice, the supernatural was the etiological theory, the theory of origins of most difficulties. Religion or magic—or both—was the medical response to such problems. This kind of thinking is not just folklore or folk belief but the prevailing medical ideology of almost all people throughout human history nearly up to the present.

☐ Exorcising a Deaf and Dumb Demon

They left that city and in the evening came to another town where a marriage ceremony was just about to begin. Satan, however, through the magical powers and spells of local sorcerers had taken away the bride's voice and she could not speak or even open up her mouth.[1]

When the bride saw Mary coming into the town carrying the Lord Christ, she came up to her, picked up the baby, and held him, hugging him tenderly and kissing him, then she bent over him and rocked him gently. Right away her tongue was freed and her ears opened wide and she could speak and hear again. She started to praise God aloud, for He had made her whole. The inhabitants of that place celebrated joyfully all that night and it seemed to them that the angels and God himself had come to be among them. The family stayed in that place for three days and were treated with great reverence and were wonderfully entertained.

Then the people of the town gave them everything they needed for traveling on and they left for a larger city where they planned to stay for a while. A woman of high status lived there who once had gone down to the river to take her bath when Satan assaulted her, took the form of a snake, and from that time on wrapped himself around her stomach and crushed her every single night.[2]

(continued on page 85)

3 | The narrative represents what then would have been common sense: if a group of people, or a little family, show up in town and the symbols of the local deities are smashed or if demons and witchcraft and diseases are overcome, it would stand to reason that the newcomers are gods. Gods represent forces "on our side" as opposed to the malevolent forces of our inhuman opponents. The Christian answer would be to affirm that yes, indeed, the baby Jesus is God incarnate, but his parents are not, and the power that seems to derive from his parents is entirely dependent on him even though he is only a few months old.

When that woman saw Mary holding the infant Christ to her breast, she asked Mary if she would let her hold Christ in her arms and kiss him. Mary agreed, and as soon as the woman picked up the baby Jesus, Satan rushed off and the woman never encountered him again. Her neighbors praised God for her and rewarded Jesus's family very generously.

A day later the woman brought scented waters in order to wash the baby Jesus and, having washed him, she kept the bathwater because she had a daughter in that town white with leprosy. When the bathwater was splashed on her and she was washed in it, she was immediately and completely cured of leprosy. The townspeople said, "Mary and Joseph and that boy are undoubtedly gods, because they do not seem at all like mortals." The girl who had been cleansed of leprosy asked to accompany them as their servant, and they agreed.[3]

. . . . .

☐ The Bridegroom Mule: A Brother Restored

The following day they departed and approached a new city, where they encountered three women returning from a graveyard crying bitterly. Mary told her servant girl, "Go ask them what is the matter, why are they weeping?"

She did, but they didn't tell her anything except to ask, "Who are you and where are you headed? It's twilight and the night will soon be here."

"We're traveling through," the girl replied, "and we're looking for an inn in order to rest for the night."

"You can come along and stay with us," they said. And so the family followed the three women into a brand new house filled with a fine variety of furnishings. The servant girl went into their living room to join the women who were, she discovered, crying as hard as they had been before. In the center of the room stood a mule covered in a beautifully embroidered silk robe with a plate of sesame in front of him and the weeping women kissed the mule as it continued feeding.

Shocked, the servant girl said, "What is the story of the mule you have here?"

The women's eyes were filled with tears as they replied, "This mule was our brother, whom our mother bore just as she bore us, his two sisters. Our father bequeathed us a very fine large estate and so, since we had only one brother, we tried our best to find a suitable bride for him to marry but a wicked and jealous girl secretly put her

(continued on page 89)

1 Stories about sorcerers or witches who magically turn human beings into animals are common throughout world folklore. Perhaps the most common such motif in our own folklore is that of the handsome prince bewitched into becoming a frog who can be transformed back only by a kiss. A Latin novel known today as *The Golden Ass,* which was written in the period 150 to 180 CE by Lucius Apuleius, tells the story of a man (supposedly Lucius himself) who accidentally turns himself into an ass through a badly concocted magical potion. Eventually, after many misadventures, Lucius is made human again through the power of the Egyptian goddess Isis.

2 It is interesting that here, as in quite a few other places in the infancy gospel traditions, all of the main characters are women. Indeed, beginning with Luke's birth account, which focuses on the excellence of Elizabeth, and Mary rather than giving praise to Zechariah and Joseph, and then moving to the stories of Anne, Elizabeth, and Mary in the Gospel of James, the infancy traditions have consistently played up or created female characters. This is, of course, particularly true of Jesus's mother Mary, who is sometimes elevated to a quasi-divine position. We might contrast their emphasis on women with the emphasis on the male characters found both in the birth narrative of the Gospel of Matthew and in the Infancy Gospel of Thomas. There men, particularly Joseph, are the predominant characters.

witch's curse on him. We, his sisters, just before dawn and while the doors of our house were securely locked, watched as he was magically transformed into the mule that you see right here in this room. We no longer have a father to turn to for help and, although we've hired the world's very best magicians and wizards to undo the spell, nothing has helped. So, whenever the grief and sadness become too much, we go off with our mother to the gravesite of our father. When we have cried our hearts out, we come back here to our home."[1]

The servant girl heard their story and said, "Be brave, don't be afraid because there's a solution to the problem already here, in your own house in fact. Once I myself had the leprosy but when I met the woman who is staying here, and the baby boy with her, Jesus is his name, my mother sprinkled water from his bath onto my skin and I became healthy again. I'm sure he can help you too, so go get my mistress Mary and ask her to come to this room. Tell her your secret and I'm sure she'll take pity on your situation."

Having heard the girl, the women quickly went to find Mary and, introducing themselves to her, sat before her and began to cry, saying, "Lady Mary, take pity on us. We have no man to be the head of our family, no father, no brother to assist us. This mule was our brother! But a woman worked witchcraft on him and made him what you see. Please help us."[2]

Mary, having compassion for the women, placed her baby on the mule's back. She said to Jesus, "Use your power to restore this mule so that he is the same man in physical form and in intelligence that he originally was." As soon as she spoke, the mule transformed into a human being, and he was a fully intelligent person again. Then he, together with his sisters and his mother, revered Mary and held baby Jesus up above their heads and kissed him, saying, "Jesus, savior of the world, your mother is blessed and blessed are our eyes that have had the chance to see you."

(continued on page 91)

3 And they lived happily ever after. There is nothing in this folktale that requires a cast of Christian characters. It is probably a tale that existed prior to the development of Christian folklore and was subsequently adapted to the story of the holy family. With stories like these, the tradition shifts farthest away from the doctrinal teaching stories that are found in the canonical gospels toward stories that are purely folklore, told for pleasure and amusement.

Both sisters told their mother, "Our brother has been brought back into human form by the Lord Jesus Christ and by the helpfulness of the girl who told us about Mary and her son. Since our brother hasn't married yet, it seems just the right thing for him to marry this girl, who has been working as a servant to Mary and Jesus."

They asked Mary what she thought about this suggestion and, after she agreed to it, the women arranged and prepared an excellent wedding. Their crying turned into laughing and their sorrow into joy and so everyone rejoiced and sang together, dressed in their best bracelets and their finest clothing. After the wedding they thanked God and said, "Jesus, son of David, you change weeping into joy and mourning into happiness!"[3]

For ten days Mary and Joseph stayed there with them, and then they went away. Everyone had shown them the greatest respect and, indeed, when Mary and Joseph departed they went home and cried, especially the servant girl.

1 In the story of Jesus's execution told in Luke's gospel (23:39–43), Jesus is crucified along with two criminals. One says to him, "If you are the Christ, save yourself and save us!" but the other says, "We are being punished justifiably, but this man has done nothing wrong." Jesus says to the latter, "Today you will be with me in paradise," and he came to be known in Christianity as the "good thief," while the former became the "wicked thief."

Titus will eventually be the "good thief" and Dumachus the "wicked thief," according to this account. However, more often the good thief is known by the name "Dismas" and the other by the name "Gestas." Neither one is named in the canonical gospels, but Dismas, here called Titus, is listed as a saint whose feast day is March 25 and whose particular concern is with prisoners.

2 This is now the second time that the infant Jesus has spoken aloud about his evidently inevitable future. The gospels of Matthew, Mark, and Luke show Jesus's fate to be something subject to some uncertainty, but later legends such as this one assume that Jesus's divinity made the course of his whole life something he knew in advance.

☐ Bandits: In Them, Jesus Sees His Destiny

Their journey continued and they entered an arid region said to be filled with bandits. Joseph and Mary decided to try and get through the area in the dark of night, but as they traveled through they saw two robbers standing watch on the road itself and a substantial number of others sound asleep nearby. The two in the road were named Titus and Dumachus, and Titus said, "Dumachus, please, let's allow these people to keep traveling on and let's be quiet so that the other men don't wake up." Dumachus refused and so Titus said again, "I promise you forty drachmas and right now you can take my belt as a sign of our deal," and before Dumachus could make a sound, Titus gave him the belt. When Mary saw how kind the robber Titus had been, she said, "God will support you with his right hand and forgive your sins."[1]

Jesus spoke up and said to his mother, "Thirty years from now the Judeans will crucify me in Jerusalem and at the same time these two thieves will be crucified too. Titus will be at my right and Dumachus on my left. From that time on, Titus will go forward into paradise."

Mary responded, "God forbid that this should happen to you!"[2]

1 This particular story falls into the category of an etiological myth because it gives a supernatural explanation for an observable fact. The explanation given in the Book of Genesis that snakes forevermore must crawl on their bellies because a snake tempted Eve is an etiological myth. Here we are told about the supernatural origin of Arabian balsam (*Commiphora opobalsamum*) in the region of Matariyya. During the medieval period, and somewhat later, Matariyya was renowned for the quality of its balsam, which was exported for use in medicinal preparations of many different types. Matariyya is near Heliopolis in Egypt, a main religious center, and so this may have been the city the narrative refers to as containing many temples.

2 This is a fascinating summary conclusion and leaves the reader wishing to know more. What happened when the holy family and the infant Jesus came into the presence of Pharaoh? We will never know, but the implication that there are many other tales and legends, stories and miracle accounts about the baby Jesus is certainly true. We are lucky to have the ones we do have.

3 The narrative appears to change here, as if one story collection had concluded and another was now added on to the end of it. Herod Archelaus was the son of Herod the Great, and when Herod died in 4 BCE, Archelaus assumed the throne under the authority and protection of Rome. However, in 6 CE his power in Judea was removed from him by Rome, which then assumed direct governance of that region through a series of procurators.

4 The story about Joseph's fear of Archelaus and, for that reason, his establishing a new home in Nazareth rather than returning to Jerusalem, is adapted from Matthew's gospel. There Joseph is warned by God in a dream, here he is warned by an angel; in the ancient world those two means of divine communication were functionally equivalent.

5 This sentence appears to be a scribal note. Scribes sometimes marked their personal reaction to texts into the manuscripts they were working on. Here it appears that a scribe's personal comment has become part of the text itself.

☐ Balsams in His Path: The Holy Child Returns

They traveled on into a city containing many temples sheltering idols of Egyptian gods and as soon as they came up to it, that city was turned into sand dunes. They went further on to where they found a sycamore tree in a place that is now called Matariyya. There, in Matariyya, Jesus made a spring of water emerge from the ground and Mary washed Jesus's clothing there. From that time on, wherever Jesus's perspiration had touched the ground, in those places plants of Arabian balsam grow.[1]

Eventually they reached the great Egyptian city of Memphis and saw Pharaoh himself! They spent three years, all told, in Egypt and Jesus performed a great many miracles there that aren't even mentioned in the Gospels of his Infancy or in the True Gospel.[2]

Finally, however, after three years they left Egypt and came to the Judean border, but Joseph didn't dare enter. He had heard that Herod died, but feared his son Archelaus, the new king, just as much.[3]

Finally he entered Judea anyway and returned for a time to Bethlehem, but an angel of God came and said to him, "Joseph, go to Nazareth and live there."[4]

It is certainly odd that the Lord of all lands should have been carried here and there through so many different regions.[5]

· · · · ·

1 Judaism in this period continued to permit polygamy and it was practiced occasionally, but polygamy was not common. Polygamy occurred more frequently among the rich than the poor; Herod the Great had several wives at once, ten altogether.

The name Cleopas is short for the Greek "Cleopatros," the feminine form of which is much better known. It means (the child of) an honored father. In the canonical story of Jesus, Cleopas appears in canonical gospels only once, Luke 24:18, where he is a disciple of Jesus walking near the village of Emmaus (about seven miles from Jerusalem) discussing Jesus's recent crucifixion with another unnamed disciple. A third man joins their conversation and they dine with him; when he blesses the bread, they discover that he is the risen Christ and he instantly vanishes.

☐ The Co-Wife's Punishment

Two women lived in Bethlehem and they were the wives of the same man. Each of the two had a son who had fallen desperately ill with fever. One of them, named Miriam, was Cleopas's mother.[1]

She carried little Cleopas to Mary and gave Mary a very elegant lovely robe. She asked Mary if she would, in return, give her just one cloth that had been used by Jesus. Mary gave one to her and she ran home, where she sewed that piece of cloth into a shirt for her son to wear. When he put that shirt on, his fever left him and he was well again, but her rival's son died. After that, the two women despised one another.

The two women customarily took turns doing the housework. One day it was Cleopas's mother Miriam's turn, and she lit a big fire in the oven, preparing to bake bread for the family. She had been kneading dough in another room and she walked off to get it in order to put it in the fire, leaving Cleopas lying there beside the oven. Spying him lying there, her rival picked him up and threw him into the hot blazing oven and then quickly ran away. When Miriam returned with the dough, she saw Cleopas laughing away happily in a cold oven. Although the oven didn't appear to have had any fire in it recently, Miriam knew that her rival had thrown Cleopas into the oven, while it was blazing hot. Taking Cleopas out of the oven his mother brought him to Mary and told Mary everything that had happened. Mary replied, "Keep quiet about it, because you could be in real trouble if you tell anyone."

(continued on page 99)

2 As in the story of the man turned into a mule, here too women are the principal characters, with men filling in background roles. As in any folktales, the reactions of the characters are highly exaggerated, but certainly antagonism between co-wives would have been real and their jealousies on behalf of their own children would have caused strong rivalries. The question of which son would be the husband's main heir would have been one of the greatest matters of concern.

3 This is a proverb put into the service of a story, which is the usual role of proverbs in traditional culture. The violence in the story, with implicit approval of the idea that God will help the one woman get revenge on the other is to be expected in a folktale. The Grimm brothers' collection of folktales from Germanic cultures are filled with stories of rivalries and violence; the wicked stepsisters' cruelty to Cinderella and the queen's attempt to poison Snow White are just two examples.

The rival wife came to the well in order to fetch water while Cleopas was playing alone nearby. She grabbed him up and dropped him down the well and then ran home. Soon a group of men came to the well for water and saw Cleopas sitting on top of the water. They were absolutely amazed and went down into the well and pulled him out. They praised God for the miracle.[2]

Cleopas's mother came for him and took him off. Crying furiously, she went to Mary and said, "Do you see what that woman, my co-wife, has done to my son? She threw him into the well and she'll soon surely succeed in killing him soon!" Mary told her, "God will see that you get revenge."

Soon the rival wife came to the well again, but this time her feet caught in the well rope and she tumbled down into the well. Men came to rescue her, but when they dragged her up they found her skull fractured, her bones broken, and that she had died miserably. This is an instance of the saying: "They dug a deep well and then they fell into the pit they made."[3]

1 Today this boy would probably be diagnosed as autistic. From the standpoint of ancient Mediterranean cultures and, for that matter, most of the world's premodern cultures, his symptoms would indicate demonic possession. From both the modern diagnostic perspective and the ancient, the boy is unable to control his actions and cannot personally be held responsible for what he does. Demonic possession as an explanation for socially unacceptable actions not only served as a medical diagnosis, it also distanced an individual from his or her actions and made the defense "the devil made me do it" the ancient equivalent of today's "not guilty by reason of insanity."

2 James and Joses, mentioned here, are listed as two of Jesus's brothers in the New Testament gospels of Mark 6:1–6, and Matthew 13:54–58. Later tradition, in respect to the doctrine of Mary's perpetual virginity, understood Jesus's brothers to be cousins or, more commonly, stepbrothers from the widower Joseph's first marriage. The idea of Joseph having children from a previous marriage enters the later tradition through the account in the Gospel of James.

3 The image of young Judas trying to bite Jesus is extraordinary. The Gospel of Luke 22:3 affirms that Judas betrayed Jesus because Satan entered into him just before the Last Supper, while John 13:27 portrays Judas as becoming possessed just after Jesus gave him a bit of bread during the Last Supper. As it often does, the Gospel of the Infancy is laying the groundwork during Jesus's childhood for events that all of its readers know will take place later in his life. In the Gospel of John 19:34 a Roman soldier (not a Judean) stabs Jesus during the crucifixion.

☐ Satan's Bite:
The Young Judas Iscariot

Another woman lived there with her son named Judas, who was possessed by Satan. Whenever Satan controlled him, he would try to bite anyone nearby and if he couldn't manage to bite someone else, he would bite his own arms and hands.[1]

The mother of this unhappy boy happened to hear about Mary and Jesus and went to them, carrying her son in her arms. Meanwhile, James and Joses had taken Jesus off to play with other children and, when they arrived at the place for play, they sat down. Judas, who had become possessed, sat down on Jesus's right. Satan, as he usually did, compelled the boy to try to bite Jesus. He couldn't do it and, frustrated, he struck Jesus so hard that Jesus started to cry. Right then, Satan left Judas and scampered off in the form of a rabid dog.[2]

That same little boy who hit Jesus and from whom Satan ran like a dog was Judas Iscariot, the one who betrayed Jesus to the Judeans. On the same side where Judas hit Jesus, Judeans later pierced him with a spear.[3]

. . . .

The Gospel of Philip coincidentally makes use of similar imagery of a dyer's shop when it says: "The Lord went into the dye works of Levi. He took seventy-two different colors and threw them into the vat. He took them out all white. And he said, 'Even so has the Son of Man come as a dyer.'" The number seventy-two traditionally refers to the number of nations on earth, and so the point of that little parable is that through the Lord Jesus, all people are united into one.

Humor is very rare in early Christian writing, but this story is meant to be funny. As Joseph goes around doing his work badly, Jesus follows repairing it and straightening things out. It is interesting that whereas Mary is always exalted and no breath of criticism is ever uttered about her, the ancient storytellers were willing to make a few critical comments about Joseph.

☐ Divine Mischief:
The Boy Jesus at Play

One day when Jesus was playing with other boys, he came running past a dyer's business where a man named Salem worked. There were many pieces of cloth there ready to be dyed in the different colors specified by their owners. Racing into the shop, Jesus grabbed all of the different pieces of cloth and threw them into a hot kettle of indigo dye.

When Salem came back and saw all of his customers' cloth dyed bright blue, he began to roar angrily at Jesus, saying, "What have you done to me, son of Mary, you've damaged my business and the clothing of our neighbors! They all wanted different colored dyes for their cloth and you've spoiled them all!" Then Jesus replied, "I'll make the cloth whatever colors you want." And right away he took pieces of cloth out of the vat of indigo dye and they were dyed the exact colors that Salem's clients had wanted." When the Judeans saw this miracle, they glorified God.[1]

Wherever Joseph went in the vicinity of the village, Jesus went with him. Joseph made milk pails, doors, gates, boxes, and all manner of wooden items. Every time that Joseph needed to make a piece of wood longer or shorter, wider or more narrow, Jesus would take hold of it, stretch out his arm, and the wood would change into the size Joseph needed. Joseph never had to make an item entirely by himself and that was fortunate, for Joseph was not a very skillful carpenter.[2]

. . . . .

(continued on page 105)

3 This too is meant to be a funny story and arises from the equation of baby goats and little children. The pun in English of "kids" for young goats and "kids" for children comes from the same idea. This folktale takes its humor both from that equation and by taking the metaphor of Jesus as the good shepherd literally.

4 In this part of the infancy gospel, which was probably once separate and later added to the tales of the holy family traveling around Egypt, we have a lot less exaltation of the divine infant Christ than we did before. This section is interested more in having fun and telling simple stories. The shape-shifting power that was used by the witch to turn a young husband-to-be into a mule is here used by Jesus just for fun.

Another day Jesus went out into the road and saw some boys playing, so he went to join them. Seeing him come they ran off, playing hide-and-seek with him. They hid away and he had to try and find them. Jesus came to the doorway of a large house and asked some women nearby where the boys had gone. They said that they'd not seen any boys, and Jesus asked, "Well what is in your big oven there?"

The women replied, teasing him, "Some young goats about three years old."

Jesus shouted, "Come on out, goats, and meet your shepherd." The boys came out, but now they were young goats leaping and jumping around Jesus. When the women saw it happen, they were astonished and frightened.[3]

They begged Jesus saying, "Lord Jesus, son of Mary, good shepherd of Israel, have mercy on your servants standing here. We believe you have come to help us, not to hurt us. Please, through your mercy, bring back the boys you transformed."

And Jesus replied, "Come out boys so we can go play." Suddenly, as the women watched, the young goats changed back into the boys that they were.[4]

1 As the previous story reflected the humorous taking-literally of the idea of Jesus as good shepherd, so this story makes a childhood game out of the claim that Jesus is the Christ, the anointed king of Israel. It might remind a reader of the mockery of the guards, at the time of Jesus's crucifixion, who dressed Jesus in royal robes and made a crown of thorns for him. The present story is the conceptual opposite of that, a crown of wildflowers instead of thorns and everything done just for fun.

2 The inclusion of precise details gives the tragedy an aura of factuality. The fact that snakes often eat eggs, especially of ground-nesting birds like the partridge, indicates that the story is based in experience.

□ The King, Christ and a Snake

In the month called Adar, Jesus was playing with the other boys. They began to pretend that he was king and so they took their coats off and laid them on the earth for Jesus to sit upon. They made him a crown to wear out of wildflowers and he put it on and then some stood to his right and his left as if they were bodyguards of a king.[1]

If anyone happened to pass by, the boys seized him and told him that he had to salute their king if he wanted to be allowed to continue on. Meanwhile, some men came by carrying a boy on a stretcher. The lad had gone out into the woods to look for partridge eggs and, finding a nest, he put his hand into it to take out eggs, only to be struck by a poisonous snake. He screamed but by the time his friends ran up to him they found him, unconscious and so they ran for help. Now he was being carried back to the village by his family.[2]

When they came to the place where Jesus was sitting pretending to be king, some of the boys who were playing at being his royal court ran off to insist that the boy bitten by the snake and his friends should come and show respect to the king. The group carrying the stricken boy refused to play along, but the other boys pulled at them and insisted that they come.

When they came up to Jesus, he asked "Why are you carrying that boy?"

"Because a poisonous snake bit him."

Jesus said, "Let's go out and kill that snake."

But the parents of the stricken boy said they couldn't possibly go because their son was dying! Jesus's companions replied, "Didn't

(continued on page 109)

3 | The Hebrew word "*qana*" means zealot and so this boy is the same person as Simon the Zealot. Christian translators going from Greek to Latin confused *qana* with "Canaan," and so the name came to be Simon the Canaanite in some traditions. In the canonical gospels, Jesus calls disciples only after he has begun his principal mission, but here he institutes discipleship at a very early age.

❖ | At this place in the Gospel of the Infancy the narrative begins to repeat the stories of the Infancy Gospel of Thomas and continues to do so all the way to its conclusion. Accordingly, we will turn our attention to the original Infancy Gospel of Thomas itself rather than follow this later retelling.

you hear what our king told you? Let's go kill that snake; didn't you hear what he ordered you to do?

So they were forced to return into the woods, carrying the stretcher, whether they wanted to or not. When they reached the partridge's nest Jesus said, "Is this where the snake is hiding?"

"Yes," they replied.

Jesus called the snake out of its hiding place and it came. Then he said to the snake, "Go take out all of the poison that you injected into that boy." The snake crawled up to the boy and removed all of its poison. Then Jesus cursed it so that it burst into pieces and died. He touched the boy and he was made healthy once again and began to cry. Jesus told him, "Stop crying, for from now on you will be a disciple of mine," and that boy grew up to be Simon the Caananite who is named in the Gospel.[3]

The Infancy
Gospel of
Thomas

1 It is not entirely clear who is meant here. The name Thomas means "twin" and in John's gospel he is called "Didymos Thomas," which means "twin" in Greek (Didymos) and "twin" in Aramaic (Thomas); Thomas is a nickname, not a proper name. In the Sayings Gospel of Thomas, which is wholly unrelated to the Infancy Gospel of Thomas, his proper name is given as Judas, a very common name of that period. The custom of claiming that anonymously circulated documents were written by well-known people was widespread in the early Christian period and so we have Paul's Letter to the Laodacians, the Gospel of Philip, the Gospel of Mary, the Secret Book of John, and many other texts that were not written by the persons indicated by their titles. The term "philosopher" today means a professional academician, but in ancient times it could be used for wise people more generally.

2 There is no chance that this author and the person nicknamed Thomas who was a disciple of Jesus are the same person. "Thomas" is a pseudonym for an unknown person writing in Greek, probably in the middle of the second century.

☐ The Introduction to the Infancy Gospel of Thomas

These are stories of the Lord's childhood from the philosopher Thomas of Israel.[1]

I, Thomas of Israel, will tell you and, indeed, all gentiles the stories of the Lord Jesus Christ's childhood, about all of the great works he performed while he was in our land.[2]

1 One of the controversial issues in contemporary scholarly study of early Christian texts is when to use the term "Jew" and when to use the term "Judean" for the people who are called "Ioudaios" in Greek. There is just one word, "Ioudaios" or, plural, "Ioudaioi" for what in English are two very different words. In English "Judean" means a person who belongs in a region and to a culture, while "Jewish" describes a person who is a member of an ethnic group who practices a particular religion. In English the word "Jew" emphasizes the religious side of "Ioudaios," while "Judean" emphasizes the regional.

As Galilee was not part of Judea, we shouldn't automatically assume that all Galileans were Ioudaioi. Here the author specifies that a character is Judean even though the infancy gospel assumes that all of the inhabitants of Nazareth are Jewish (to use the English language distinctions). Perhaps some of the people of Nazareth were immigrants from Judea into Galilee and so were Judeans by their ethnic and national origins.

☐ Clay Sparrows: A Dark Miracle

Here my stories begin:

On one Sabbath day little Jesus, when he was a child of five, was playing at the edge of a creek at the place where the water becomes shallow. There were a lot of other children there playing with him. He ordered the water to flow into little pools and become clear, and it happened. With that soft clay he made a dozen little clay sparrows.

But a Judean who saw how Jesus was playing on the Sabbath went to Joseph and told him, "Down at the creek your son is making toy birds out of clay. This is a sort of work and it's forbidden on the Sabbath day." Joseph walked down to the creek and said, "Why are you doing things on the Sabbath that aren't allowed?"[1]

(*continued on page 117*)

2 This is a nice little story and it prefigures difficulties that the canonical gospels describe when they tell stories of times that Jesus worked miraculous cures on the Sabbath. When he was criticized for doing so, he famously said "The Sabbath was made for human beings, not human beings for the Sabbath" (Mark 2:27), which may well be more of a Galilean than a Judean view of the strictness required in Sabbath observance. Jesus was condemned for healing on the Sabbath on the grounds that healings that could wait one more day should not be carried out on the day of rest; healings immediately necessary to save a life were not only allowed on the Sabbath, they were also commanded and required by Judean Torah law.

The story of the clay birds is found twice in the Qur'an. In the Qur'an 3:49 Jesus says, "I have brought you a sign from your Lord. I shall create something in the shape of a bird for you out of clay, and blow into it so it will become a real bird, with God's permission." Then, in Qur'an 5:110 God says about Jesus that he "created something out of clay looking like a bird with my permission; you breathed into it, and by my permission it became a bird!" From this we know that Muhammad heard tales found in the Infancy Gospel of Thomas from Christians whom he met.

3 Most readers today are shocked that stories like this one ever circulated about Jesus. But ancient Christians thought of God as a more awesome being than most modern Christians do. God was a source of dangerous power and of awe-inspiring royal potency, and to anger God would be perilous indeed. When they thought of this huge cosmic power embodied in an immature boy, they thought of the dangers he might pose for the people around him. In later Christian piety the infant Jesus—for example, the Infant of Prague—was nothing but innocence and sweetness, goodness and benevolence. But in the first century Christians had a more natural opinion of what would happen if the reins of maturity and adulthood were absent from God's incarnation.

Jesus immediately clapped his hands and shouted, "Fly away!" to the clay birds and they became living sparrows that flew away chirping. The Judeans who saw this happen were astonished and reported to their leaders what they had seen Jesus do.[2]

The scribe Annas's son took a willow branch and broke down the little pools of water Jesus had made. All the water flowed back into the creek and Jesus, furious, said, "You ungodly fool, what harm were my pools of water doing to you? You, dry up like a dead tree that can't grow leaves or fruit or roots." And the boy completely withered up.

Jesus went home to Joseph's house as the boy's parents, crying with grief, came up to Joseph and blamed him, saying, "You're at fault for having a child who does this sort of thing."[3]

1 This story shows how some of the Christians of the second century thought a little boy of four or five years old, with the power of God, would act. The idea that he would always be good and kind and so forth was more a dreamy wish than a reasonable outcome. Those who invented these folktales were imagining what it would have been like if, in a real rural village, a boy were to possess powers of this sort before he was old enough to know how to use them.

2 Here, when Jesus speaks, there are significant problems in the wording because various manuscripts differ significantly. Evidently, scribes found certain passages quite unpalatable and made various confusing attempts to repair and modify them. Note that Jesus is depicted as isolated and alienated from the villagers with whom he lives and may even be isolated in his own home because he realizes that the father with whom he lives is not his true Father at all. Even in the canonical story about Jesus's childhood found in the Gospel of Luke, there is a hint of alienation when Jesus tells his mother and his father, who have been frantically worrying about him, thinking him lost, that they should have known he'd be away from them in the Temple going about his true Father's business (Luke 2:48–50).

☐ The Vengeful Boy: Christ in Conflict

Another time Jesus was walking through the village of Nazareth and a child, running along, banged into Jesus's shoulder. Jesus said angrily, "You'll go no further," and immediately the child dropped dead.

The people who had seen this said, "Why was this child Jesus ever born? When he says something, right away it happens."

The boy's parents held Joseph responsible and they ran to him saying, "You can't go on living here with a child like that! You have to teach him to bless people and to stop cursing them. He's killing our children!"[1]

Joseph took little Jesus aside and scolded him, saying, "Why are you doing things that make your neighbors suffer so? Now they're furious at us." Jesus answered, "These aren't your own words and so I'm not going to be angry with you. But the people who told on me will be punished." Instantly, all of those who had accused Jesus were struck blind.

Bystanders were amazed and puzzled and remarked that everything Jesus said came to pass in a miraculous way. When Joseph saw that Jesus had blinded so many people, he grabbed Jesus by the ear and pulled it painfully. The child was furious and said, "If they come seeking, they won't find. You're acting very stupidly. Don't you know I'm not really your boy? Leave me alone!"[2]

(continued on page 121)

3 While this is obviously a folktale and a naïve one at that, it does address a rather interesting question: What would you do if you had to educate God into the nuances of human society? How can God be educated, if God knows everything already? What if God's knowledge is perfect on the divine level, but not perfect in terms of learning to be human? The story here features the need to socialize God into a community of human beings. Today's view of Jesus is that he was perfect in every way from the beginning and had no "learning curve" at all, but eighteen hundred years ago people were not so sure that it would be easy for the incarnate God to discover how to be a human being. Zacchaeus offers not just to teach Jesus to read and write but also to develop the social skills and respect for others that are required for successful social existence.

4 Again, the problem is that Jesus as the incarnate Son of God does, in some sense, know everything, but yet, on the other hand, he has difficulty relating to other human beings. Here he humiliates his teacher, but expresses supernaturally perfect intellectual understanding of his letters. The manuscripts of this passage are all disrupted when it comes to what it was Jesus taught about the alpha. He seems to have described it geometrically, and perhaps he did so in a way that made the geometric structure of the letter symbolize Christian concepts such as the holy trinity, but it's impossible to be sure and the version written here is just a guess.

A teacher named Zacchaeus overheard Jesus saying these things and he was shocked that such a young boy would speak this way to his own father. Several days later he approached Joseph and said, "I would like to teach this very intelligent child of yours. I'll teach him to read beginning with the alphabet, and I'll teach him to be polite and to salute his elders and to be kind to the other children.³

Zacchaeus taught Jesus the Greek alphabet from alpha to omega, but when he asked Jesus questions about the first letters, Jesus responded, "If you don't know about these letters, if you don't even know alpha, how can you teach beta?" Then Jesus taught Zacchaeus all about alpha, describing it in great detail, saying, "Alpha has two ascending lines meeting at the elevated apex and dancing together there, and it has a triangle of three equal angles outlined beneath that apex point formed by a single vertical stroke through the ascending lines, and it has two unattached lines at its lower extent forming two angles and it is all well related and balanced so long as the initial lines are of equal length." Further, he outlined its allegorical implications, and all of this astonished Zacchaeus, who couldn't think of anything to say back to him.⁴

(continued on page 123)

5 Zaccaeus's lament here falls into a standard rhetorical category of ancient writing, and the extreme despair he expresses isn't meant to be taken too seriously. The passage contrasts with the concluding story in the Infancy Gospel of Thomas where, following Luke's account, a more mature Jesus respectfully learns from and questions and teaches the Temple elders in Jerusalem.

6 This section of the infancy gospel reflects several motifs found in the Gospel of John. For example, the idea that Jesus does all and only what his Father sent him to do can be found throughout that gospel. It is in John's account that Jesus says, "For judgment I came into this world, that those who do not see may see, and that those who see may become blind" (John 9:39). Note that Jesus now does heal and restore everyone injured in earlier parts of the infancy gospel, but also note the realistic reaction of the villagers to him. The Infancy Gospel of Thomas does take seriously the problem of how a community might have responded to the presence of an immature incarnate God in their midst, and they are not yet ready to trust that he has become mature enough to handle his powers reliably.

Zacchaeus, Jesus's teacher, was amazed at hearing such a description and so many allegorical explanations of alpha from little Jesus and so he said to those nearby, "Oh dear, I am stunned. This little child shames me and I cannot stand his stern gaze, nor can I fully understand him. Joseph, take him away! Nothing I say to him comes out clearly and I'm not even sure he is from this world. Maybe he's from the time before the world began! I don't know from what sort of woman he comes from. I'm dumbfounded because, while I thought he'd be my student, now he's my master. Oh the shame of it, being old and here I am about ready to faint and die because of this little boy. I can't even look him in the face because he's overcome me so completely. Compared to him I can't say a thing intelligently about the letter alpha and as for the alphabet, I don't know the start or the finish of it compared to him. Joseph, my brother, just take him away back to your house. He's something special but I don't know whether he is some sort of god or angel or what. I just don't know."[5]

As the Judeans tried to soothe Zacchaeus, Jesus laughed out loud and said, "Now let the blind see that I have come from above both in order to curse and to bring heavenly things to your minds. I'm doing what the One who sent me told me to do." As soon as Jesus stopped talking, at that moment everyone who had been cursed became well and the blind became able to see clearly again. But still, no one in the village risked making him angry for fear that he might curse or wound them.[6]

1 This story marks a change in the infancy gospel's portrayal of Jesus. Having established some of the dangers involved in having an immature divine person in the village, the infancy gospel portrays the villagers as frightened to have Jesus around. Naturally, therefore, Jesus becomes suspect even when he has had nothing to do with a situation. Now, in the story, people suspect Jesus but his role is evolving into that of a healer sometimes falsely accused, but one with courage enough to face down his accusers and prove them wrong. He raises the boy and his reputation begins to change; he is no longer killer but savior.

2 Here the local reaction to Jesus continues to shift from fear to awe. Now Jesus begins to heal not just as evidence of his own innocence, but simply to help another person. Nazareth villagers are beginning to see his divine nature as a blessing and not as a threat. The villagers suspect now that Jesus has a holy spirit dwelling in him, that he is a human being but with the added presence of a divine power.

☐ The Young Healer Explores His Powers

Soon afterwards, Jesus was playing upstairs on the roof of a particular house when one of his playmates fell all the way down to the ground and died. When they saw it happen, the other children ran off, but Jesus remained behind. The dead boy's parents came and were furious with Jesus, accusing him of pushing the boy so that he fell. Jesus jumped down from the roof next to the body and shouted, "Zeno," which was the boy's name, "Get up and tell me whether or not I pushed you?" The boy rose up and said, "Absolutely not, Lord, you didn't push me down but you raised me up." Everyone who saw this was astounded and even the boy's parents were praising God because of the miracle and they revered Jesus.[1]

Shortly after that, a young man was cutting firewood when his ax slipped, sliced open his foot, and he lay dying from the loss of blood. There was a tremendous uproar, people came running to the site, and Jesus came running too. Jesus pushed his way through the throng, took hold of the dead boy's foot, and he immediately came back to life. Jesus told him, "Rise up, split the wood and remember me." The crowd of people who had seen what had taken place revered Jesus and said, "The Spirit of God certainly lives in this child."[2]

1 Evidently the earlier stories in the Infancy Gospel of Thomas all took place when Jesus was five years old. Now he is six. Like the miracle involving clay birds flying, carrying water in a porous cloth would be categorized as a "nature miracle," one that involves a breach in natural law. Jesus's reaction to the broken pot is simple and not aggressive; earlier in the narrative he might have struck back at whomever broke his pot, but by this time he is more in control of himself. The sudden appearance of Mary in the narrative reminds a reader that, for the most part, she has been absent and that the primary actors in the narrative have been boys or men. The idea of Mary storing the memory of the miracle is reminiscent of Luke's comment that after Jesus was born and the shepherds and the angels appeared, "Mary kept all these things, and pondered them in her heart" (Luke 2:19).

2 Here, for the first time in the narrative, Jesus shows a special interest in the less fortunate and uses his miracle working power to benefit them especially. The narrative has traced the evolution of his understanding of his divine power one step further. Note that he is now eight years old, as this narrative tells it, and so his ability to cope with his special power continues to evolve.

3 This is a simple story of another nature miracle and it assumes that Jesus was raised by Joseph the carpenter. The idea that Joseph was a carpenter arose because when Matthew revised Mark's Gospel to produce his own, he changed Mark's phrase "the carpenter (*tekton*) son of Mary" in Mark (6:3) into the phrase "the son of Mary and the carpenter (*tekton*)" (Matthew 13:55). This is all we know from the canon about "Joseph the carpenter" and so folklore began to fill in some details.

□ Divine Carpenter:
Jesus Adjusts His Elder's Mistakes

Once, when Jesus was six years old, his mother gave him a water pot and sent him to the well to bring home water. As he went through the crowd that gathered by the well his pot struck against someone else's pot and his shattered. Jesus took off his shirt, filled it up with water, and brought it home to his mother. When Mary saw the miracle that had just happened she kissed Jesus and stored the memory of this event alongside the other miracles she had seen.[1]

In the spring, when it was time to sow, the child went out into the field with his father to sow the wheat. Jesus only sowed one single handful but when he harvested what he had sown, and after he had threshed it all, it had produced a hundred measures of wheat. Jesus invited the poor to come and he gave them all of his. What was left over, Joseph took home. This happened when Jesus was eight years old.[2]

Joseph the carpenter usually made wooden ploughs and yokes, but once a wealthy man put in an order for a bed. Joseph made a bed, but discovered at the end that one of the two sidepieces was too short. He couldn't think of any solution to the problem. Then Jesus said to his father, "Put the two boards side by side and hold one end of the shorter board," and, after Joseph complied, Jesus took the other end of the shorter board, pulled on it, and it stretched to be the same length of the other piece. Joseph was amazed when he saw Jesus do this and he embraced his son, kissed him, and said, "I am blessed because God gave this boy to me."[3]

1 In terms of the story the Infancy Gospel of Thomas is telling, this seems to be a regression back to the younger, dangerous, and vengeful Jesus. Here, though, he is reacting to being struck whereas earlier he reacted to accidental slights. In any event, in real life children do not evolve year after year to be better and better in every way; they do occasionally slip and revert to behaviors they appeared to have outgrown.

2 This is now the third variant of the teacher story. In folklore we should expect every retelling of a story to be somewhat different and expect that a collection of tales might have the same one in more than one variation. It is very common, in folklore throughout the world, for an important motif or story to be repeated three times. The threefold repetition may serve to emphasize the contrast between Jesus in his childhood years and the more mature boy Jesus who appears in the Temple politely teaching and learning from his elders, in the concluding section of the Infancy Gospel of Thomas.

A village thinking itself "threatened" by a very young Jesus might find that as he gradually matures, he nevertheless continues to constitute a threat. It seems that courage is required to deal with him. Note that Joseph, the teachers, and Mary are somewhat more sympathetically portrayed characters than is Jesus himself, who seems to have dangerous and unpredictable power. We might give the authors of the Infancy Gospel of Thomas some credit for imagining realistically what it might have been like to encounter an immature incarnation of the all-powerful God in village streets.

Of all the scriptural gospels, it is the Gospel of John that most strikingly conveys the image of Jesus as a powerful being from a different realm walking on earth. Indeed, in that gospel Jesus said to the people around him, "You are from below, I am from above; you are of this world, I am not of this world," (John 8:23). Throughout John's gospel Jesus is "not of this world" in his words and in his powers, nor is he entirely of this world in the Infancy Gospel of Thomas.

☐ The Pupil Teaches His Teacher

Because Jesus was becoming more mentally mature, and his intelligence was becoming more evident, Joseph continued to think that he should learn to read and so he entrusted him to a teacher who said, "I'll teach him the Greek alphabet first, and after that the Hebrew alphabet." This teacher was aware of the problems that Jesus's first teacher had encountered and he was frightened.

However, he wrote down the alphabet and taught the letters to Jesus for a long time, but Jesus didn't say a word. Finally Jesus said, "If you're a competent teacher and know the letters so well, tell me all about the alpha. Then I'll tell you all about the beta."

The teacher, offended, was furious and slapped Jesus on the head painfully and Jesus, responding, cursed him so that he passed out and fell face-first to the ground. The child went back home and Joseph, who was now very angry, ordered Mary to make sure that he stayed indoors, and said to her, "Don't let him go outside because if anyone makes him angry they might die."[1]

Sometime later one of Joseph's friends, a teacher, came to Joseph and said, "If you bring your child to my school, I think I can talk him into learning to read." Joseph replied, "If you've got the courage for it, go ahead and take him along with you."[2]

3 The narrative has changed from portraying Jesus as a little boy who knows everything about the alphabet and the alphabet's symbolism, which are things taught to the youngest boys, to portraying Jesus as an older boy who now knows about the scripture of divine Torah law through the Holy Spirit. Again, note that the presence of the Spirit is assumed here to account for Jesus's special abilities.

4 Joseph, like the other villagers of Galilee, is not confident yet that the young Jesus is mature enough to hold back his power, and so Joseph fears that he might have hurt the teacher. But Jesus is becoming more confident and more controlled as he becomes older. In ancient biographies—and this is a series of folktales in biographical form—the most significant facts about a person reveal that person's character. Now, as he becomes more mature, Jesus's character as one full of wisdom and goodness is becoming clear to some of those who come to know him. This development is moving the narrative toward the point where it can come to an end, so that the story of the adult Jesus in the canonical scriptures can begin.

So, scared nearly to death, the teacher walked along with Jesus, who went with him quite happily. When they entered the school building Jesus noticed a book open on the lectern, picked it up, but rather than read it, he began to preach in the power of the Holy Spirit, teaching God's law to everyone who was there.[3]

Gradually, a considerable crowd assembled and listened and they were all impressed by the quality of his message and how well-spoken he was, even though he was still a very young man.

Joseph heard what was happening and worried that Jesus might be endangering his friend. He ran to the school building, fearing that the new teacher might not be capable of handling the situation. But the teacher told Joseph, "I accepted your boy as my pupil, but he's already full of wisdom and goodness, so please take him home."

Young Jesus, hearing this, laughed out loud, saying, "You are absolutely right, you understand, and so for you I'll cure the other teacher." He did so and that teacher rose up healthy again. Then Joseph took Jesus back to their home.[4]

1 In historical fact there was a brother of Jesus named James (Mark 6:1–3) who became the leader of the Christian church in Jerusalem after Jesus's death. James was the principal Christian leader of the early church and so came into conflict with Paul, especially regarding the extent to which Jewish Christians were expected to follow Jewish religious law (Acts 21:17–25). James, who had acquired the nickname "the righteous," was executed in 62 CE on the orders of the high priest Ananus.

2 Note that Jesus touches the infant; he doesn't just speak to it. The neighbors' reactions are now changing to positive ones as Jesus's actions no longer seem so threatening to them. Jesus is still a child, but now he is behaving as a divinely benevolent child.

Again the neighbors speculate about Jesus. Is he God? Does the Holy Spirit dwell in him or is he a special person of a different category altogether, one who has descended from heaven? Is he an angel? The people of Nazareth are shown to be growing in their understanding of Jesus's nature; the stories do not show them immediately and miraculously understanding. Earlier the people supposedly said, "The Spirit of God certainly lives in this child," assuming that his powers are not his own but that they are due to an indwelling divine being. Now they are said to speculate that he might himself be God, or at least an angel of God. This shift in interpretation accurately reflects the evolution of Christological thinking during the first century.

3 Jesus's power over death impresses the villagers most, and this completes a full narrative circle, for in the beginning his neighbors had reason to fear that he would bring death to them; now they know Jesus as someone who can save them and many others from death. The Christology of the villagers is shown to be advancing toward what the Christian religion teaches. The short narrative called the Infancy Gospel of Thomas has more development and structure to it than some might think.

☐ The Miraculous Physician

One day Joseph sent his son James out to gather up firewood, and little Jesus came along behind. As James picked up dry branches, a poisonous snake bit him. He was in agony and nearly dead when Jesus came up, blew on the snakebite, and the pain ended. The snake burst open and James went back home safe and sound.[1]

A little baby recently born to one of their neighbors became ill and subsequently died. Jesus heard the mother crying and weeping aloud, ran to her, and, discovering the dead infant, touched its chest and said, "I'm telling you not to die but to live and to stay with your mother." Immediately, the baby looked up at him and laughed. Jesus said to the mother, "Pick it up and give it milk and remember me." The people of the village who had crowded around were amazed and said, "Surely this boy is a God, or an angel of God, for everything he says comes true." Jesus ran off to play with the other children.[2]

Sometime later, as a house was being built, there was a great turmoil and when Jesus heard it he went to investigate. He found a man dead there and, taking him by the hand, said, "I say: 'Arise! And go on working,'" and so the man did, and he revered Jesus. When they saw what happened, the villagers were again astonished and they said, "This boy must have come down from heaven because he's saved so many people who died, and he'll continue to do so all his life long."[3]

1 This account is very similar to the story in the Gospel of Luke 2:41–52. In the earlier village-teacher stories Jesus responded very poorly to instruction and his divine knowledge overcame any deference to adult authority. Now, older and more mature, he hears teaching and questions the authorities, evidently in a deferential and polite manner even though his knowledge does exceed theirs.

The ancient historian Josephus, in his autobiography, bragged of his own attainments in words that remind one of this story about Jesus. Josephus, who was born in 37 CE and died circa 100 CE claimed that by the time he was fourteen years old, the high priests and others learned from him, and influential men frequently came to him to find out his opinion on difficult points of Torah law. Josephus seems to have been a little too impressed with himself.

☐ In the House of My Father: Jesus in the Temple

At the age of twelve Jesus and his parents went, as was customary, along with many others, to Jerusalem to celebrate the Passover festival. When Passover ended, they were returning home when Jesus suddenly went back into Jerusalem. His parents didn't realize that he had gone. After another full day's journey back toward Galilee they started looking for their son among their friends and relations but couldn't find him anywhere. They began to be frightened and went back to the city hoping to find him. Finally, after three days, they did find him in the Temple, surrounded by teachers, and he was hearing God's law as they taught it and he was questioning them about it. All the men listened to him carefully and were amazed that a boy that young could make the Temple's elders and teaches fall silent through his explanations of the main points of God's law and of the prophets' words.[1]

Mary came up to him and said, "Why did you do this to us, we've been frantically looking all over for you?"

Jesus replied, "Why were you looking for me? You should have known that I'd be in the house of my Father."

The Pharisees and scribes who were there asked Mary, "Are you this boy's mother?"

She said that she was, and they said, "Blessed are you among women, because God has blessed the fruit of your womb. We've never before seen or even heard of a lad with so much wisdom and goodness."

(continued on page 137)

2 Here, in a sense, the Infancy Gospel of Thomas concludes. But in another sense, it doesn't end but rather connects to the canonical Gospel of Luke from which the Infancy Gospel of Thomas's conclusion is drawn.

These stories give a background to Jesus's career that is lacking in the canonical sources. In its somewhat clumsy way, the Infancy Gospel of Thomas tries to show how a little boy who is God in a village environment learns through some trials and errors to control and make benevolent use of his powers on earth. Now that Jesus is more mature, the Gospel of Thomas can come to a close with passages borrowed from Luke's gospel. It thereby makes way for the full story of Jesus found in Luke's entire gospel that itself segues into the history of the Christian church as told in Luke's Acts of the Apostles.

Jesus got up, followed his mother, and again was under the care of his parents. His mother paid careful attention to all of the things that had happened. Jesus continued to develop in his stature, wisdom and goodness. To him be glory forever. Amen.[2]

☐ Notes

Foreword

1. Raymond E. Brown, Karl P. Donfried, Joseph A. Fitzmyer, and John Reumann, eds. *Mary in the New Testament*. New York: Paulist Press, 1978, 248–49.

2. Joachim and Anna were also frequently invoked in the West. Prior to the Second Vatican Council it was quite common for young Catholic women seeking a husband to pray to the grandmother of Jesus ("Saint Ann, get me a man, as fast as you can").

3. See Mary B. Cunningham, "The Use of the Protoevangelion of James in Eighth-Century Homilies on the Mother of God," in Brubaker, Leslie and Mary Cunningham, eds. *The Cult of the Mother of God in Byzantium*. Aldershot, UK: Ashgate, 2009. Cunningham herself translated many of these homilies in *Wider than Heaven: Eighth-Century Homilies on the Mother of God*. Crestwood, NY: St. Vladimir's Seminary Press, 2008.

4. Palamas, Gregory. *Mary the Mother of God: Sermons by Gregory of Palamas*. Translator Christopher Veniamin. South Canaan, PA: Mount Thabor, 2005.

5. Although this work is traditionally attributed to Pope Gelasius (492–96), the first three chapters may go as far back as Pope Damasus I (366–84). Chapters 4 and 5 were added in the late fifth or sixth century (probably in Gaul), including the listing of apocryphal books like the Protoevangelion.

Introduction

1. In Greek texts Mary's mother's name is "Anna" and that is the name that is used in Eastern churches today. Therefore, the sign within Mary's Jerusalem birthplace mentions Anna not Anne. However, the English equivalent is "Anne" and so she is known as St. Anne throughout the English speaking Catholic world and churches in her name are St. Anne's. The name in Hebrew would have been "Hanna," which can also be spelled "Hannah."

2. Miller, Robert. *Born Divine: The Births of Jesus and other sons of God*. Santa Rosa, CA: Polebridge Press, 2003.

3. Schaberg, Jane. *The Illegitimacy of Jesus: A Feminist Theological Interpretation of the Infancy Narratives*, Expanded Twentieth Anniversary Edition. Sheffield, England: Sheffield Phoenix Press, 2006.

4. The Sayings Gospel of Thomas is a list of 114 sayings attributed to Jesus that was discovered in Nag Hammadi Egypt in 1945. It is an important document for study of the teachings of Jesus, but it has nothing to do with the Infancy Gospel of Thomas except for the fact that coincidentally it has the same name.

5. Hock, Ronald. *The Infancy Gospels of James and Thomas*. Santa Rosa, CA: Polebridge Press, 1995.

6. Davies, Stevan. *The Gospel of Thomas: Annotated and Explained*. Woodstock, VT: SkyLight Paths, 2002.

7. Hock, Ronald. *The Infancy Gospels of James and Thomas*. Santa Rosa, CA: Polebridge Press, 1995.

8. Smid, Harm Reinder, trans. G. E. van Baaren-Pape. *Protoevangelium Jacobi: A Commentary*. Assen, The Netherlands: Van Gorcum, 1965.

9. Wake, William, William Hone and Jeremiah Jones, eds. *The Apocryphal Books of the New Testament*. Philadelphia, PA: David McKay Publisher, 1901. Being all the gospels, epistles and other pieces now extant attributed in the first four centuries to Jesus Christ, his apostles, and their companions not included, by its compilers, in the authorized New Testament.

10. Roberts, Alexander and James Donaldson eds. *Ante-Nicene Fathers. Volume 8: Fathers of the Third and Fourth Centuries*. 1886. Reprint, Grand Rapids, MI: Eerdmans, 1975.

11. James, Montague R. *The Apocryphal New Testament, Being the Apocryphal Gospels, Acts, Epistles, and Apocalypses*. Oxford, UK: Clarendon Press, 1924.

12. Hennecke, Edgar, and Wilhelm Schneemelcher eds. *New Testament Apocrypha: Volume One, Gospels and Related Writings*. Translator R. McL. Wilson. Philadelphia, PA: The Westminster Press, 1963.

13. Cowper, B. Harris. *The Apocryphal Gospels and Other Documents Relating to the History of Christ Translated from the Originals in Greek, Latin, Syriac, Etc. with Notes, Scriptural References and Prolegomena*. London: Williams and Norgate, 1867.

14. Cartlidge, David and David Dungan. *Documents for the Study of the Gospels*. Minneapolis, MN: Fortress Press, 1994.

☐ Suggestions for Further Reading

Brown, Raymond. *The Birth of the Messiah*. Anchor Bible Series (updated), Garden City, NY: Doubleday, 1999.

> An exhaustive scholarly commentary on the canonical birth narratives, with some reference to the apocryphal stories as well. It is hard to imagine a more thorough study of these narratives. Father Brown would not rule out the historicity of much of the tradition.

Byrne, Matthew. *The Way It Was: The Narrative of the Birth of Jesus*. Dublin, Ireland: Columba Press, 2005.

> This book will be of particular interest to more conservative Christians who want a discussion of the canonical birth stories placed in the cultural and historical setting of ancient times.

Davies, Stevan. *The Gospel of Thomas: Annotated and Explained*. Woodstock VT: Skylight Paths, 2002.

> If you are curious about the Sayings Gospel of Thomas as well as the Infancy Gospel of Thomas, you will find this commentary and translation of interest.

———. *The Revolt of the Widows: The Social World of the Apocryphal Acts*. Carbondale IL: Southern Illinois University Press, 1980.

> This is my study of the Christian folk narratives that tell of the miracles and adventures of Jesus's apostles. These stories were written at roughly the same time as the folk narratives in the infancy gospels.

———. *The Secret Book of John: The Gnostic Gospel—Annotated and Explained*. Woodstock, VT: SkyLight Paths, 2005.

> The most significant and influential text of the ancient Gnostic religion tells the story of how God fell from perfect Oneness to imprisonment in the material world, and how we can reverse God's descent and find our salvation.

Freed, Edwin. *The Stories of Jesus' Birth: A Critical Introduction*. London: T&T Clark, 2004.

> Those who want a thoughtful, sympathetic, yet critical look about the canonical gospels' stories of Jesus's birth will enjoy this book.

Fitzmyer, Joseph. *The Gospel According to Luke I–IX: Introduction, Translation, and Notes*. Anchor Bible Series. Garden City, NY: Doubleday, 1982.

> This is a full and thorough a commentary on the birth narratives in Luke's gospel. It is accessible to lay readers and takes a view sympathetic to the concerns of Christian believers.

Hennecke, Edgar, and Wilhelm Schneemelcher. *New Testament Apocrypha: Gospels and Related Works*. Vol. 1. Translated by R. McL. Wilson. Philadelphia: Westminster Press, 1963.

This collection of translations gives a full overview of the Christian tradition of stories outside the canonical texts. The translations are accompanied by high-level academic introductions.

Hock, Ronald. *The Infancy Gospels of James and Thomas*. Santa Rosa, CA: Polebridge Press, 1995.

This is a fine scholarly edition of the infancy gospels for nonspecialist readers. It gives the Greek and English in side-by-side translations, and in copious notes Hock discusses both the nuances and the variations in the Greek manuscripts. He also gives his own views regarding aspects of the texts.

Irving, T. B. *Noble Qur'an: Arabic Text and English Translation*. Beltsville, MD: Amana Publications, 1991.

This is the translation of the Qur'an used in this book. Unlike many other translations, it is written in clear English and without archaisms.

Miller, Robert. *Born Divine: The Births of Jesus and Other Sons of God*. Santa Rosa, CA: Polebridge Press, 2003.

In this fascinating study of the birth stories about Jesus (but very little about other sons of God), Miller makes a sustained, important argument that the concept we have of the virgin birth of Jesus is not present in Matthew's gospel, and that later generations have read it into that story. Miller's case will make any reader rethink some long-standing presuppositions.

Miller, Ron. *The Gospel of Thomas: A Guidebook for Spiritual Practice*. Translated by Stevan Davies. Woodstock, VT: SkyLight Paths, 2004.

An innovative guide that brings a new spiritual classic into daily life. This guidebook is written for readers of all religious backgrounds.

Schaberg, Jane. *The Illegitimacy of Jesus: A Feminist Theological Interpretation of the Infancy Narratives*. Expanded 20th Anniversary Ed. Sheffield, England: Sheffield Phoenix Press, 2006.

Schaberg argues that Jesus was illegitimate and that Mary may have been impregnated by a human male against her will. She takes much of the canonical scripture's accounts to be historically valuable, but reads them quite differently than others have done. Her presentation is interesting and academically thorough.

Smid, Harm Reinder. *Protevangelium Jacobi: A Commentary*. Translated by G. E. van Baaren-Pape. Assen, The Netherlands: Van Gorcum, 1965.

This is a very detailed commentary on the Greek text of the Protevangelium, the best such commentary that has ever been produced. It is, however, quite technical and will be of interest primarily to professional scholars.

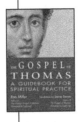

Prayer / Meditation

Sacred Attention: A Spiritual Practice for Finding God in the Moment
by Margaret D. McGee
Framed on the Christian liturgical year, this inspiring guide explores ways to develop a practice of attention as a means of talking—and listening—to God.
6 x 9, 144 pp, HC, 978-1-59473-232-4 **$19.99**

Women Pray: Voices through the Ages, from Many Faiths, Cultures and Traditions
Edited and with Introductions by Monica Furlong
5 x 7¼, 256 pp, Quality PB, 978-1-59473-071-9 **$15.99**

Women of Color Pray: Voices of Strength, Faith, Healing, Hope and Courage *Edited and with Introductions by Christal M. Jackson*
Through these prayers, poetry, lyrics, meditations and affirmations, you will share in the strong and undeniable connection women of color share with God.
5 x 7¼, 208 pp, Quality PB, 978-1-59473-077-1 **$15.99**

Secrets of Prayer: A Multifaith Guide to Creating Personal Prayer in Your Life *by Nancy Corcoran, CSJ*
This compelling, multifaith guidebook offers you companionship and encouragement on the journey to a healthy prayer life. 6 x 9, 160 pp, Quality PB, 978-1-59473-215-7 **$16.99**

Prayers to an Evolutionary God
by William Cleary; Afterword by Diarmuid O'Murchu
Inspired by the spiritual and scientific teachings of Diarmuid O'Murchu and Teilhard de Chardin, reveals that religion and science can be combined to create an expanding view of the universe—an evolutionary faith.
6 x 9, 208 pp, HC, 978-1-59473-006-1 **$21.99**

The Art of Public Prayer: Not for Clergy Only *by Lawrence A. Hoffman*
6 x 9, 288 pp, Quality PB, 978-1-893361-06-5 **$18.99**

A Heart of Stillness: A Complete Guide to Learning the Art of Meditation
by David A. Cooper 5½ x 8½, 272 pp, Quality PB, 978-1-893361-03-4 **$16.95**

Meditation without Gurus: A Guide to the Heart of Practice
by Clark Strand 5½ x 8½, 192 pp, Quality PB, 978-1-893361-93-5 **$16.95**

Praying with Our Hands: 21 Practices of Embodied Prayer from the World's Spiritual Traditions *by Jon M. Sweeney; Photographs by Jennifer J. Wilson; Foreword by Mother Tessa Bielecki; Afterword by Taitetsu Unno, PhD*
8 x 8, 96 pp, 22 duotone photos, Quality PB, 978-1-893361-16-4 **$16.95**

Silence, Simplicity & Solitude: A Complete Guide to Spiritual Retreat at Home
by David A. Cooper 5½ x 8½, 336 pp, Quality PB, 978-1-893361-04-1 **$16.95**

Three Gates to Meditation Practice: A Personal Journey into Sufism, Buddhism, and Judaism *by David A. Cooper* 5½ x 8½, 240 pp, Quality PB, 978-1-893361-22-5 **$16.95**

Prayer / M. Basil Pennington, ocso

Finding Grace at the Center, 3rd Ed.: The Beginning of Centering Prayer *with Thomas Keating, ocso, and Thomas E. Clarke, sj; Foreword by Rev. Cynthia Bourgeault, PhD*
A practical guide to a simple and beautiful form of meditative prayer.
5 x 7¼, 128 pp, Quality PB, 978-1-59473-182-2 **$12.99**

The Monks of Mount Athos: A Western Monk's Extraordinary Spiritual Journey on Eastern Holy Ground *Foreword by Archimandrite Dionysios*
Explores the landscape, the monastic communities, and the food of Athos.
6 x 9, 256 pp, 10+ b/w drawings, Quality PB, 978-1-893361-78-2 **$18.95**

Psalms: A Spiritual Commentary *Illustrations by Phillip Ratner*
Reflections on some of the most beloved passages from the Bible's most widely read book. 6 x 9, 176 pp, 24 full-page b/w illus., Quality PB, 978-1-59473-234-8 **$16.99** HC, 978-1-59473-141-9 **$19.99**

The Song of Songs: A Spiritual Commentary *Illustrations by Phillip Ratner*
Explore the Bible's most challenging mystical text.
6 x 9, 160 pp, 14 b/w illus., Quality PB, 978-1-59473-235-3 **$16.99**; HC, 978-1-59473-004-7 **$19.99**

Sacred Texts—SkyLight Illuminations Series

Offers today's spiritual seeker an accessible entry into the great classic texts of the world's spiritual traditions. Each classic is presented in an accessible translation, with facing pages of guided commentary from experts, giving you the keys you need to understand the history, context and meaning of the text. This series enables you, whatever your background, to experience and understand classic spiritual texts directly, and to make them a part of your life.

CHRISTIANITY

The End of Days: Essential Selections from Apocalyptic Texts—
Annotated & Explained *Annotation by Robert G. Clouse*
Helps you understand the complex Christian visions of the end of the world.
5½ x 8½, 224 pp, Quality PB, 978-1-59473-170-9 **$16.99**

The Hidden Gospel of Matthew: Annotated & Explained
Translation & Annotation by Ron Miller
Takes you deep into the text cherished around the world to discover the words and events that have the strongest connection to the historical Jesus.
5½ x 8½, 272 pp, Quality PB, 978-1-59473-038-2 **$16.99**

The Lost Sayings of Jesus: Teachings from Ancient Christian, Jewish, Gnostic and Islamic Sources—Annotated & Explained
Translation & Annotation by Andrew Phillip Smith; Foreword by Stephan A. Hoeller
This collection of more than three hundred sayings depicts Jesus as a Wisdom teacher who speaks to people of all faiths as a mystic and spiritual master.
5½ x 8½, 240 pp, Quality PB, 978-1-59473-172-3 **$16.99**

Philokalia: The Eastern Christian Spiritual Texts—Selections Annotated & Explained *Annotation by Allyne Smith; Translation by G. E. H. Palmer, Phillip Sherrard and Bishop Kallistos Ware*
The first approachable introduction to the wisdom of the Philokalia, which is the classic text of Eastern Christian spirituality.
5½ x 8½, 240 pp, Quality PB, 978-1-59473-103-7 **$16.99**

The Sacred Writings of Paul: Selections Annotated & Explained
Translation & Annotation by Ron Miller
Explores the apostle Paul's core message of spiritual equality, freedom and joy.
5½ x 8½, 224 pp, Quality PB, 978-1-59473-213-3 **$16.99**

Sex Texts from the Bible: Selections Annotated & Explained
Translation & Annotation by Teresa J. Hornsby; Foreword by Amy-Jill Levine
Offers surprising insight into our modern sexual lives.
5½ x 8½, 208 pp, Quality PB, 978-1-59473-217-1 **$16.99**

Spiritual Writings on Mary: Annotated & Explained
Annotation by Mary Ford-Grabowsky; Foreword by Andrew Harvey
Examines the role of Mary, the mother of Jesus, as a source of inspiration in history and in life today. 5½ x 8½, 288 pp, Quality PB, 978-1-59473-001-6 **$16.99**

The Way of a Pilgrim: The Jesus Prayer Journey—Annotated & Explained
Translation & Annotation by Gleb Pokrovsky; Foreword by Andrew Harvey
This classic of Russian spirituality is the delightful account of one man who sets out to learn the prayer of the heart, also known as the "Jesus prayer."
5½ x 8½, 160 pp, Illus., Quality PB, 978-1-893361-31-7 **$14.95**

Sacred Texts—cont.

MORMONISM

The Book of Mormon: Selections Annotated & Explained
Annotation by Jana Riess; Foreword by Phyllis Tickle
Explores the sacred epic that is cherished by more than twelve million members of the LDS church as the keystone of their faith.
5½ x 8½ , 272 pp, Quality PB, 978-1-59473-076-4 **$16.99**

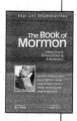

NATIVE AMERICAN

Native American Stories of the Sacred: Annotated & Explained
Retold & Annotated by Evan T. Pritchard
Intended for more than entertainment, these teaching tales contain elegantly simple illustrations of time-honored truths.
5½ x 8½, 272 pp, Quality PB, 978-1-59473-112-9 **$16.99**

GNOSTICISM

Gnostic Writings on the Soul: Annotated & Explained
Translation & Annotation by Andrew Phillip Smith; Foreword by Stephan A. Hoeller
Reveals the inspiring ways your soul can remember and return to its unique, divine purpose.
5½ x 8½, 144 pp, Quality PB, 978-1-59473-220-1 **$16.99**

The Gospel of Philip: Annotated & Explained
Translation & Annotation by Andrew Phillip Smith; Foreword by Stevan Davies
Reveals otherwise unrecorded sayings of Jesus and fragments of Gnostic mythology.
5½ x 8½, 160 pp, Quality PB, 978-1-59473-111-2 **$16.99**

The Gospel of Thomas: Annotated & Explained
Translation & Annotation by Stevan Davies Sheds new light on the origins of Christianity and portrays Jesus as a wisdom-loving sage.
5½ x 8½, 192 pp, Quality PB, 978-1-893361-45-4 **$16.99**

The Secret Book of John: The Gnostic Gospel—Annotated & Explained
Translation & Annotation by Stevan Davies The most significant and influential text of the ancient Gnostic religion.
5½ x 8½, 208 pp, Quality PB, 978-1-59473-082-5 **$16.99**

JUDAISM

The Divine Feminine in Biblical Wisdom Literature
Selections Annotated & Explained
Translation & Annotation by Rabbi Rami Shapiro; Foreword by Rev. Cynthia Bourgeault, PhD
Uses the Hebrew books of Psalms, Proverbs, Song of Songs, Ecclesiastes and Job, Wisdom literature and the Wisdom of Solomon to clarify who Wisdom is.
5½ x 8½, 240 pp, Quality PB, 978-1-59473-109-9 **$16.99**

Ethics of the Sages: Pirke Avot—Annotated & Explained
Translation & Annotation by Rabbi Rami Shapiro Clarifies the ethical teachings of the early Rabbis. 5½ x 8½, 192 pp, Quality PB, 978-1-59473-207-2 **$16.99**

Hasidic Tales: Annotated & Explained
Translation & Annotation by Rabbi Rami Shapiro
Introduces the legendary tales of the impassioned Hasidic rabbis, presenting them as stories rather than as parables. 5½ x 8½, 240 pp, Quality PB, 978-1-893361-86-7 **$16.95**

The Hebrew Prophets: Selections Annotated & Explained
Translation & Annotation by Rabbi Rami Shapiro; Foreword by Zalman M. Schachter-Shalomi
Focuses on the central themes covered by all the Hebrew prophets.
5½ x 8½, 224 pp, Quality PB, 978-1-59473-037-5 **$16.99**

Zohar: Annotated & Explained *Translation & Annotation by Daniel C. Matt*
The best-selling author of *The Essential Kabbalah* brings together in one place the most important teachings of the Zohar, the canonical text of Jewish mystical tradition.
5½ x 8½, 176 pp, Quality PB, 978-1-893361-51-5 **$15.99**

About SKYLIGHT PATHS Publishing

SkyLight Paths Publishing is creating a place where people of different spiritual traditions come together for challenge and inspiration, a place where we can help each other understand the mystery that lies at the heart of our existence.

Through spirituality, our religious beliefs are increasingly becoming a part of our lives—rather than *apart* from our lives. While many of us may be more interested than ever in spiritual growth, we may be less firmly planted in traditional religion. Yet, we do want to deepen our relationship to the sacred, to learn from our own as well as from other faith traditions, and to practice in new ways.

SkyLight Paths sees both believers and seekers as a community that increasingly transcends traditional boundaries of religion and denomination—people wanting to learn from each other, *walking together, finding the way.*

For your information and convenience, at the back of this book we have provided a list of other SkyLight Paths books you might find interesting and useful. They cover the following subjects:

Buddhism / Zen	Global Spiritual	Monasticism
Catholicism	Perspectives	Mysticism
Children's Books	Gnosticism	Poetry
Christianity	Hinduism /	Prayer
Comparative	Vedanta	Religious Etiquette
Religion	Inspiration	Retirement
Current Events	Islam / Sufism	Spiritual Biography
Earth-Based	Judaism	Spiritual Direction
Spirituality	Kabbalah	Spirituality
Enneagram	Meditation	Women's Interest
	Midrash Fiction	Worship

Or phone, fax, mail or e-mail to: SKYLIGHT PATHS Publishing
An imprint of Turner Publishing Company
4507 Charlotte Avenue • Suite 100 • Nashville, TN 37209
Tel: (615) 255-2665 • www.skylightpaths.com
Prices subject to change.

**For more information about each book,
visit our website at www.skylightpaths.com**

Printed in the USA
CPSIA information can be obtained
at www.ICGtesting.com
LVHW010358160824
788375LV00005B/94

9 781594 732584